SEEKING THE KINGDOM

The Sermon on the Mount Made Practical for Today

SEEKING THE KINGDOM

The Sermon on the Mount Made Practical for Today

DAVID S. DOCKERY
& DAVID E. GARLAND

Harold Shaw Publishers
Wheaton, Illinois

Unless otherwise noted, Scripture has been taken from *The Holy Bible: New International Version*. Copyright 1973, 1978, 1984 by the International Bible Society. Used by permission of Zondervan Publishing House. Scripture marked NEB has been taken from *The New English Bible*, copyright © the delegates of the Oxford University Press and the syndics of the Cambridge University Press, 1961, 1970. Reprinted by permission. Scripture marked RSV has been taken from the *Revised Standard Version* of the Bible, copyrighted 1946, 1952, © 1971, 1973 by the Division of Christian Education of the National Council of Churches, U.S.A. and is used by permission. Scripture marked KJV has been taken from the *King James Version* of the Bible.

ISBN 0-87788-756-X

Library of Congress Cataloging-in-Publication Data

Dockery, David A.
Seeking the kingdom : the Sermon on the mount made practical for today / David S. Dockery, David E. Garland
p. cm.
Includes bibliographical references.
ISBN 0-87788-756-X
1. Sermon on the mount—Criticism, interpretation, etc.
2. Bible. N.T. Matthew V-VII—Criticism, interpretation, etc.
I. Garland, David E. II. Title.
BT380.2.D63 1992
226.9'06—dc20 92-4937
CIP

---

99 98 97 96 95 94 93 92

10 9 8 7 6 5 4 3 2 1

In loving memory of
W.A. Huckeba
(1915-1992)
who invested his
life "seeking
first the Kingdom
of God"
Matthew 6:33

CONTENTS

Preface

The opportunity to write a studyguide commentary on the Sermon on the Mount has been a most rewarding experience for us. We have been challenged afresh to "seek first the kingdom" in all areas of our lives. Such a command is not to be taken lightly. Certainly it is easier to write about the meaning of the Sermon than it is to live out its meaning in our fallen world. We accept both the privilege to study these most significant words of Jesus and the responsibility to obey as well. We trust the readers will likewise experience the joy of hearing these teachings anew while seeking God's enabling grace to put these things into practice.

We have written this book primarily for laypeople, though we hope pastors and students will also find it useful. Study questions and action steps appear at the conclusion of each chapter to help readers focus on key themes and issues. This format also serves to make the book "user-friendly" for group study and discussion.

It is our hope that believers from various traditions and theological and denominational communities will be able to find help and direction when studying this book in connection with the Sermon on the Mount. However, we hope the book especially will help those churches and individuals in the Southern Baptist Convention who will together study the Sermon in years to come. We also pray that the book will be a trustworthy guide for many others in months and years to come.

It is always the case that many people other than the authors are involved in the publication of a book. This work is no exception. We wish to offer our sincere thanks to Stephen Board at Harold Shaw Publishers for his invitation to us to write this book. We also wish to thank Ramona Cramer Tucker and the editorial staff for their capable preparation of the manuscript. We offer a special word of appreciation for the sacrificial love and support of our families during this process.

Above all, we wish to express our gratitude to our Lord and Savior, Jesus Christ, for the opportunity to study his words in the Sermon on the Mount and to serve in his kingdom.

Soli Deo Gloria

David S. Dockery
David E. Garland

The teaching

of the

Sermon on the Mount

is not to be admired

but to be obeyed

R.T. France

1

WHAT IS THE SERMON ON THE MOUNT?

Matthew 5:1-2

The Sermon on the Mount is perhaps the most prominent feature of what many consider to be the most important book ever written, the Gospel of Matthew.

No other religious teaching in the history of humanity has attracted as much attention as the Sermon on the Mount. Philosophers and political leaders like Mohandas Gandhi and others who have refused to believe in Jesus as the Christ, the Lord and Savior, have, nevertheless, admired and tried to follow his teachings in the Sermon. It has received such titles as the Christian Magna Charta, the Christian Manifesto, the Design for Life, or simply Ethics for Christian Living. These designations clearly point to the importance granted to this portion of Scripture in the history of the church.

The Context of the Sermon

The Sermon on the Mount is the first of five great discourses in Matthew (Chapters 5–7; 10; 13; 18; 24–25). Three basic types of material are employed: (1) beatitudes or declarations of blessedness; (2) ethical admonitions; and (3) contrasts between Jesus' ethical teaching and prevailing traditions.

Matthew first introduces us to Jesus with a genealogy (1:1-17), an account of his miraculous conception by the Holy Spirit, and later adoption by Joseph (1:18-25), and his flight to Egypt and return to Galilee (2:1-23). These things establish Jesus to be the Messiah, the son of David (1:1). Matthew then reveals Jesus to be the obedient Son of God in the account of his baptism by John the Baptist (3:17) and his temptation by the devil (4:3, 6, 8-9). He then tells us that Jesus went about all Galilee teaching in the synagogues and preaching the gospel of the kingdom (4:23). Now in chapters 5–7 the reader gets the opportunity to listen in on that teaching. The Sermon on the Mount is the first close-up picture of Jesus in our New Testament. Here we see him going up a mountain, the place of revelation, to teach his disciples about life under the reign of God.

This teaching from the mount contains Jesus' most unforgettable, most formidable, and most uncompromising demands. It begins, however, with good news: "Blessed are you." The ones whom no one would have considered favored are said to be especially blessed by God. God's grace will be showered on the poor in spirit, the mourners, the meek, and those who hunger and thirst for righteousness. Rejoice and be glad, Jesus says. But God's gift of grace is not to be taken for granted. Jesus instructs those who respond to this grace on how to live. God has blessed you; now here is what you are to do.

Jesus must have electrified the gathering when he told them that unless their righteousness exceeded that of the zealous scribes and Pharisees they would not have a chance of entering into the kingdom of Heaven. They must have gasped when he announced, "You have heard it said . . . but I say to you. . . ." Their hearts must have been stabbed when he shook them from their moral complacency by saying that even looking at a woman with lust is the same as committing adultery with her. He must have sparked puzzlement when he said, "If your right eye causes you to sin, pluck it out; if your right hand causes you to sin, cut it off." They must have laughed at his cartoon of a person with a plank in his eye trying to remove a particle of sawdust from someone else's eye.

They probably went away with his teaching still reverberating in their heads and hearts. His teaching is worded so that it not only sticks in the mind but calls for decisive obedience. This is indicated by the Sermon's ending: a short parable stresses the importance of practicing what has just been taught (7:24-27) and the crowd expresses amazement at the authority with which Jesus speaks (7:28-29).

So far, in Matthew's account, only four disciples have been called. But Matthew understands the audience to consist of more than just four fishermen, since the crowds are said to marvel at the conclusion of the Sermon (7:28-29). Crowds from every point on the compass have flocked to Jesus (4:25). When Jesus sees the crowds he retreats to a mountain where he schools those who want to follow him as disciples in the kingdom lifestyle. The exact location of the mountain remains uncertain. It may have been the sloping hillside at the northwest corner of the Sea of Galilee, not far from Capernaum (see Luke 6:17). The new words for kingdom living, like the old, are given from a mountain (see Matt. 17:1, 9; 28:16), perhaps in comparison and contrast with Mount Sinai (see Exod. 19:1-2).

The Setting and Structure of the Sermon

Opinions differ whether the Sermon is to be understood as a summary of Jesus' teachings from numerous occasions or whether it is one sermon preached at one sitting. Matthew possibly took a single sermon and expanded it with the use of other relevant teachings of Jesus. As a master teacher Jesus would probably not expect his listeners to absorb so much ethical instruction at one time. Thirty-four of the 107 verses in Matthew's account are not found in Luke's record of the event (Luke 6:20-49) but are scattered throughout Luke in other contexts. Forty-seven of Matthew's verses have no parallel at all in Luke. It appears that Matthew, consistent with his style elsewhere, arranged the Sermon's material in a topical and orderly manner.

The Sermon on the Mount is carefully structured. The nine beatitudes (5:3-12) and the salt and light metaphors (5:13-16) make up the introduction. The thesis statement on the greater righteousness required of kingdom citizens is found in 5:17-20. This is further explained by contrasting Jesus' teaching with other legal material (5:21-48). Genuine piety is expounded by means of three examples in 6:1-18. Chapter six, verses 19-34, focuses on issues of security and true riches. Chapter seven, verses 1-12, deals with relationships: how kingdom citizens should teach others. The Sermon's concluding section (7:13-27) shows the readers there are only two possible responses. The three illustrations all emphasize the need for commitment. The last statement (7:28-29) points to Jesus' authority as a teacher.

Interpreters have understood this message in a variety of ways. The literature on the Sermon is vast. One survey has identified over thirty different approaches to the Sermon.

What follows is a brief description of some of the more prominent ones.

Approaches to the Sermon

Utopian ideal

Jesus' words in the Sermon on the Mount are incomparable, but some say they are also impossible. Many have protested that the Sermon contains "too high an ideal for ordinary mankind, and even too high for the man of more than average calibre."[1] They charge that the directions found in the Sermon can only work in a Utopia where humans are not riddled with sin. They do not work in real life. As a result, many have attempted to modify Jesus' radical demands to make them practical.

Millennial ethic

Some have limited the teaching of the Sermon to the future millennial kingdom that Jesus offered to the Jews, but which they rejected so that it was postponed until after his second coming. This approach sees the Sermon as intended for kingdom citizens but fails to see the kingdom as already inaugurated. The kingdom, in this interpretive framework, will not be instituted in any way until after the Second Coming. Yet, the type of society requiring commands against murder, adultery, divorce, and so on, can hardly be described as millennial.

A common sense guide

One approach to applying the commands of the Sermon on the Mount, consciously or unconsciously, modifies them so that they conform to common sense. Certainly, Jesus did not mean for us to take everything he said literally! Does he really want us to pluck out our eyes and throw them away when they cause us to sin? If so, there would be a lot of one-eyed or blind Christians. Common sense tells us that Jesus is using exaggeration to catch our attention and drive home the grave nature of sin. He wanted to dramatize the necessity of total commitment to God. We are to cut off the influences that lead us to sin.

But there is a danger in first passing Jesus' teachings through the filter of our common sense; it can screen out the radical command. It may result in our cutting the demands of Jesus down to our size. Common sense tells us, for example, to strike back when someone hits us, not to turn the other cheek. Common sense tells us not to give to every person who begs of us and to audit carefully anyone who wants to borrow. Common sense tells us that anxiety for what we should eat and wear is prudent. Who else is going to worry about us if we do not? Common sense challenges many of Jesus' instructions and argues that the issues are more complicated than what Jesus pictures.

The problem with this approach is that our common sense might deceive us. How do we distinguish the commandment of the Lord from our own personal opinion about what he "really" meant? How do we know that Jesus did not intend for his disciples to do exactly as he said? He certainly did not invite us to pick and choose from his teachings what we want to obey and what we want to disregard. The teaching offered in the Sermon on the Mount is not a cafeteria line from which we can make selections according to our particular tastes.

Binding on all or a committed few?

Another approach to the demands found in Jesus' Sermon is historically related to Roman Catholicism. At one time, scholars distinguished between "precepts" binding on all and "evangelical counsels" required only of the clergy. This view assumed that only a few could or would even try to obey the commands. Therefore, they were considered binding on only the most devoted Christians, the "cream of the crop."

This way of handling the teachings in the Sermon on the Mount is at least realistic in admitting that some Christians are more willing than others to make sacrifices for their faith. But it creates a double standard among disciples. It says that some commands are valid for the elite but not for others. It allows the so-called "run-of-the-mill" Christian to ignore most of what Jesus says. But Jesus does not make any such distinctions in the Sermon. He addresses one and all.

Teaching for the end times

Some modern readers have argued that Jesus anticipated the end of the world was at hand with the dawning of the kingdom of God. They have concluded that Jesus' ethical teaching was conditioned by that impending end. They claim that the Sermon on the Mount was intended to be operative only during the exceptional situation of catastrophe that would mark the passing of this world. Of course one would be willing to give to those who beg and borrow with no questions asked if the end were at hand. What would money matter then?

But the Sermon on the Mount contains no hint that Jesus intended it to be heard only as a set of emergency procedures valid only for the brief time before the end. It is not an "interim ethic"; it is an eternal ethic.

The Sermon gives every indication that Jesus is concerned about our anger, lust, truthfulness, hatred, and use of money *in the present*. It seems clear that he means to give his disciples instructions for their behavior right here and now. He says: This is what you do when someone slaps you. This is what you do when someone comes to borrow from you. This is what you do when you give alms, pray, and fast. He also says that everyone who hears these words of his and does them is like a wise man who builds his house upon rock. When the deluge comes, the one who has listened and obeyed will be ready. If one waits to build a house on rock in the middle of the deluge, it will be too late. Jesus expected his commands to be obeyed now, not later.

Internal attitudes

Others argue that Jesus is not concerned with specific acts but only with internal attitudes. Jesus does not require that we actually go into a broom closet to pray. He is concerned that we approach God reverently and not use devotion time to show off our piety. The danger of this approach can be seen when we turn his saying to go the extra mile into a general principle. The radical nature of this command in Jesus' context is softened. For most, going the extra mile means giving an extra effort. But, as we shall see below, this reading misses entirely what Jesus was saying. When we turn Jesus' commands into general principles, we are at risk of watering them down.

Showing our need for mercy

Others have claimed that the main purpose of the Sermon on the Mount is to bring us to repentance so that we can see how unworthy we really are. This approach assumes that what is contained in the Sermon on the Mount is an attainable ethical goal. The teaching is intended to show us how far short we fall in meeting God's requirements, and it points the way to the only one who has fulfilled the commands. Martin Luther said that after reading the Sermon on the Mount everyone looks pretty poor in spirit.

It is true that no one can feel very smug after reading through the Sermon. But when one has repented and entered the kingdom of God, what then? How is one to live? The Sermon on the Mount offers specific guidelines for life for those who have already repented. This emphasis is clear from Jesus' instruction, "Do not be like them!" (6:2-5, 16). He is talking about a particular lifestyle and particular actions that he expects of his disciples.

Kingdom Living Here and Now

After we have made every attempt to find some loophole that allows us to escape the awesome demands that we find in the Sermon, we can only conclude that Jesus gave us this teaching so that it would be obeyed, not admired. The commands found in the Sermon on the Mount, therefore, should be taken with the utmost seriousness. Jesus considered them obligatory on all citizens of the kingdom. The words of General Omar Bradley in an Armistice Day address in 1948 bear repeating: "We have grasped the mystery of the atom and rejected the Sermon on the Mount." We can reject or ignore the Sermon on the Mount only at great peril. It contains the unconditioned expression of God's will for how the kingdom citizen is to live. It is a charter of conduct for disciples.

While we may find the demands overwhelming, we need to recognize that grace surrounds the Sermon on the Mount. Just prior to the Sermon, Jesus preaches the good news of the kingdom and heals every disease and infirmity among the people (4:23-24). Immediately after the Sermon, Jesus heals a leper, a centurion's servant, Peter's mother-in-law, and all the sick and demon possessed who come to him from the surrounding countryside (8:1-17). Matthew underscores this by quoting Isaiah 53:4. This is the one who takes our infirmities and bears our diseases, including our sins (8:17).

The Sermon itself begins with an announcement of God's grace. Throughout we see evidence that the kingdom has indeed been inaugurated, but not yet consummated. The beatitudes are not entrance requirements for the kingdom, since they contain no imperatives. They are pronouncements of the blessings of the age to come on those who are in distress. The poor in spirit, the mourners, the meek, and the persecuted had hoped for God's deliverance. Jesus announces that deliverance has come. The obedience required by Jesus in the Sermon on the Mount is therefore a response to the grace already received from God. The Sermon on the Mount outlines the responsibilities of those who accept this grace presented to us in Christ (7:13-16). With the offer of grace comes a summons and a command. After the beatitudes, the emphasis falls on hearing and doing (5:19; 7:24-27), on works (5:16), and on bearing fruit (7:15-23). There are also dire warnings about the failure to obey.

If we start by asking the question, "How can we possibly measure up to Christ's commands?" we will get one answer. But it will be misleading. If we ask the questions, "What is God's will?" and, "How does God expect us to live?" we will get another answer. Jesus does not say, "Do what you can and forget about the rest." He lays before us God's absolute pattern for our lives.

Despite the objections of those who say it is impossible to live out what is taught here, the Sermon is not a charter of despair. We might compare Jesus' instructions to the strictures placed on a diabetic child. To protect the child's health, he is told that he can no longer raid the refrigerator after school but needs to watch his diet carefully. Twinkies, doughnuts, and double jelly sandwiches are out. But one day you catch the child coming out of the kitchen with jam all over his face. What are the parents to do? To exaggerate things, the parents could say: "We gave the rules a try but they didn't work. The child disobeyed. It was too much to expect of the child. We will forget about the rules and let the child eat whatever he wants." One option for the parents is to throw out the rules. But the consequences will be deadly for their child.

Another even more far-fetched alternative is to keep the rules and throw out the child. The parents could say, "The child broke the rules, therefore we will give the child the boot."

More reasonably, the parents could determine to keep the standards and the child. This last option is decidedly what our heavenly Father does. It is important to recognize that what Jesus offers his disciples in the Sermon on the Mount are not oppressive rules. The good Physician has prescribed these guidelines for our spiritual health. Jesus knows firsthand our weaknesses, but he also knows our needs. And the precepts in the Sermon on the Mount grow out of our needs. If we do not even attempt to meet the conditions, it will kill us. Anger, lust, hatred, revenge, hypocrisy, greed, and anxiety—the things that Jesus addresses in the Sermon—can only destroy people. And we live in a world where all these things are at home. Jesus seeks to check these lethal attitudes.

If we interpret what is contained in the Sermon on the Mount as prescriptions to help us recover and grow in our moral and spiritual health, then we can only conclude that we must strive to obey them. We should not be deterred by questions about whether this is practical or not. When someone is on the target range, for example, the only legitimate thing to shoot at is the target. One cannot say that "since I am unable to hit the target I will aim at something closer in my range." The question of the practicality of this teaching did not arise for Matthew—only for later Christians. The assumption is that these commands are not only possible, they must be obeyed.

First, these commands of Jesus must be obeyed because of the authority of the one who gives them. As a teacher, Jesus is presented as one who has authority greater than the scribes (7:28-29) and as one who is even greater than Moses, "you have heard it said . . . but I say to you" (5:21-48). Jesus closes all loopholes, including those that are culturally accepted, and intensifies the demand of the law with his insistence on a greater righteousness (5:21-22). As Immanuel, God with us, Jesus has come to fulfill the Law and the prophets (5:17) and to teach us what to do.

Second, these commands are to be obeyed because we will finally have to answer to Jesus. Jesus sits to teach in Matthew 5:1 (13:1-2; 24:3; and 26:55). In the future he will sit on a throne to reign (19:28; 25:31). He implies that he will be the judge in the last day when many will cry to him, "Lord, Lord" (7:21-23). The disciples' ultimate destiny therefore depends on their relationship to him (7:21-23) and their obedience to his words (7:24-27). Obedience is rewarded by inclusion in the kingdom of heaven (5:20); disobedience will meet with final punishment (5:22, 25-26, 29-30; 7:13, 19, 23, 27). We should not forget, however, that the Sermon on the Mount is addressed to sinners, not to flawless angels. We are taught to pray for the forgiveness of our sins. Our only hope is the mercy and grace of God.

Questions for Further Reflection

1. What is the Sermon on the Mount?

2. What is the best way to interpret the Sermon?

3. Did Jesus preach the Sermon to tell people how to become Christians or how disciples should live as kingdom citizens?

4. How do we often attempt to evade the uncomfortable directness of the Sermon on the Mount?

➠ Action Step

Read the Sermon (Chapters 5–7) in one sitting. Try reading it in a modern translation or paraphrase. Imagine hearing these words for the very first time from the lips of Jesus. What are your impressions?

2

THE CHARACTER AND INFLUENCE OF KINGDOM CITIZENS

Matthew 5:3-16

We have all received the advertisement pitch in the mail that announces, "Congratulations! You may already be a winner in the big sweepstakes." Our hearts might skip a beat as we indulge in the fantasy of winning the jackpot, but reality quickly jolts us out of our reverie. We know that the chances of having the right number are a million to one and that the whole thing is just a come-on to get us to buy something we probably don't need.

The Character of Kingdom Citizens (5:3-12)

When Jesus pronounced people blessed on the top of that mountain, it also must have caused his listeners' hearts to skip a beat. To call someone blessed was the same as offering them congratulations. Jesus saluted those he says are going to inherit the kingdom of God. Congratulations! Happy are you! It must have sounded fantastic to them.

Kingdom blessings: the beatitudes

There is a big difference, however, between the greetings we receive from the sweepstakes office and the congratulations extended by Jesus. First, the stakes are more glorious. Can one even compare the kingdom of God with the paltry, earthly award offered by the adman? Second, Jesus announces good news with no strings attached. Anyone who fits the categories of poor in spirit, mourning, meek, hungering and thirsting for righteousness, and merciful is pronounced blessed. You are already a winner. But the biggest difference is the fact that Jesus' announcement is not a come-on. The euphoria created by this surprising good news will not wear off when reality begins to set in. According to Jesus, reality itself is changing. The reign of God is invading the world through his ministry and words. God is acting decisively in the world, and things will never be the same again. Jesus' hearers are to be congratulated because they are in on the ground floor of this new existence.

Beatitudes in the world of Jesus. To understand better the significance of Jesus' offer of congratulations to his listeners, we might compare his beatitudes with other blessings in the ancient world. As "Congratulations!" are familiar in our world, so the word "blessed" was a familiar affirmation in the secular Greco-Roman world. Blessedness was something associated with the existence of the gods. Everyone assumed that the gods were blessed because they were immune to the troubles and sorrows of day-to-day existence. Any human who was thought to enjoy the imagined privileges of the gods was considered to be blessed like the gods. People were therefore saluted for their fortunate external conditions. They were called blessed if they had a beautiful home, fine children, knowledge, wealth, honor, and fame. These kinds of things reflected basic human desires and what most people thought made for the "good life." The blessed were those who luxuriated in the lifestyles of the gods—or we would say today, the lifestyles of the rich and famous.

The beatitudes found in the Old Testament are quite different from these secular blessings. People are proclaimed blessed because of their godly lives. They are to be congratulated because they have divine approval. For example, those who are pronounced blessed are those who have God as Lord (Ps. 144:15), who fear God (Ps. 112:1-3; 128:1-4; Prov. 84:12), who trust in God (Ps. 84:12), who dwell or take refuge in God (Ps. 2:12; 84:4), and who wisely obey God (Ps. 119:1-2; Prov. 8:32-34; Isa. 56:1-2). The Old Testament beatitudes are primarily intended to motivate others to develop the same sterling virtues in their lives so that they might also have God's approval. These beatitudes offer practical wisdom for happiness in this life. If you want to have lasting joy in this world, obey God.

By the time of Jesus, Israel's political situation in the world had changed dramatically for the worse. The house of David had been smashed by the Exile. Pagan enemies ruled the roost. The faithful were subjected to cruel persecution and seemed to be on the verge of extinction. The focus of the beatitudes found in the Jewish literature composed during this time between the Testaments reflects the change in these historical circumstances. The concern shifts from how to be happy in this life—which seemed impossible—to how to be happy in the life to come. The emphasis was on how to be saved from the Last Judgment. The blessed are those who will have a share in the next age. The tone of these beatitudes is therefore one of consolation and assurance. They provide encouragement in times of terrible distress by affirming that God will eventually deliver the faithful from their earthly nightmare.

Jesus' beatitudes are a bugle call that the new age of salvation has already dawned. Sirach looked back to bygone days and considered those blessed who had seen Elijah (the noncanonical *Book of Sirach* 48:11). The psalms of Solomon looked to the future and pronounced those blessed who will be born in the days of Messiah. They will be the ones who will see the good fortune of Israel and the good things of the Lord (a pre-Christian work, *Psalms of Solomon* 17:44; 18:6). The Gospels inform us that Elijah has come (Matt. 17:11) and that the Messiah is in our midst. Therefore, Jesus does not address a past generation nor a future one. He tells his disciples that they are the blessed ones because they are able to see and hear what the prophets and the righteous longed to see and hear (Matt. 13:16-17; Luke 10:23-24). He acclaims the poor in spirit, the weeping, those hungry and thirsty for righteousness, the persecuted, and the hated because God has acted decisively to make them happy. Despite appearances to the contrary, congratulations are in order because Jesus' presence fulfills all the hopes of the pious. Although the persecuted may still be harassed, they are to know that their redemption has come. Jesus announces that if our lives are marked by the characteristics of those described in the beatitudes we are already a part of the reign of God that burst in at his incarnation. "Blessed are you," he says.

The paradoxical nature of Jesus' beatitudes. Before examining the beatitudes individually, we should note one important characteristic about them. As announcements of congratulations, many of the beatitudes are paradoxical. Jesus' beatitudes do not reflect the conventional wisdom of a world that so prizes earthly well-being. He says, "Happy are those the world considers unhappy." The poor in spirit, the mourners, the meek, the hungry, and the persecuted are not normally counted as blessed. Most would view them as the unfortunate. G. H. R. Horsley writes that "poverty, humility, suffering" would never have been "morally recommended in classical culture."[1] The same may be said for our culture today.

Our society holds material blessedness no less dear than did the ancient world. We prefer to be the winners. We consider them to be the ones who are blessed. And we can tell a winner by his or her looks, status, or assortment of exotic possessions. Many people devote their whole lives trying to attain this "blessed" state of material prosperity. Our world, therefore, salutes the world beaters and the well-off, not the peacemakers and the penniless. But Jesus hails the folks that our society identifies as losers and informs them that they should be fully conscious of divine blessing. Jesus does not save them from suffering but pronounces them blessed in the midst of suffering. Despite appearances, these are the people who enjoy divine favor, and that is the only kind of blessedness that counts for anything. The early Christians were conscious that their blessed condition had nothing to do with their outward estate. That firm conviction enabled them to rejoice in their misfortunes and to endure hardship nobly (James 1:2).

Blessed are the poor in spirit (5:3)

The first four categories of those blessed all begin with the letter "p" in Greek. In English, one might capture this alliteration by translating them, blessed are the *poor* in spirit, blessed are the *plaintive*, blessed are the *powerless*, and blessed are those who *pine* for righteousness. One commentator points out that while we call this the Sermon on the Mount, it starts out spiritually in the valley. "It starts with those who feel very unlike mountains."[2] But God can only pour his blessings on those who are not too full of themselves.

Who are the poor in spirit? If one compares the first beatitude in Matthew 5:3 with the first in Luke 6:20, one immediately spots a difference. In Matthew, Jesus pronounces "the poor in spirit" blessed. In Luke, it is simply "the poor." To understand this difference and what Jesus has in mind, we need to look at the Old Testament context of the term "poor."

In the Greco-Roman world, the "poor" simply applied to those who lived in material poverty. In the Old Testament, however, the term "poor" had a religious aspect as well as referring to economic privation. The "poor" were the humble pious who were beloved by God (Isa. 61:1). One might ask, why the link between poverty and piety? The answer is that an empty purse did not allow the needy to be pushy or haughty. The poor had no material resources, no security. They were easily exploited by the rich who were characterized by their arrogance and self-sufficiency. Those who were helpless and who knew they were helpless could not rely on their financial muscle but had to wait on God. All they could do was place their lives in the hands of God.

The poor had not ceased from the land in the time of Jesus. In fact, they had increased in numbers. Their vulnerability forced them to look to God for everything. They were people like Jesus' parents, Mary and Joseph, like Anna and Simeon, like the widow with only two mites to her name. They were what James, the brother of our Lord, called "the poor of this world, rich in faith" (James 2:5).

With this background, we can see that Matthew's version, "poor in spirit," is basically identical to Luke's "poor." The phrase "poor in spirit" makes it clear that Jesus is not exalting poverty as something that is blessed in itself. It is not. Nor is Jesus suggesting that poverty creates greater spiritual depth. "The poor in spirit" are those who live in humble acknowledgment of their impoverishment before God. In Hebraic idiom, the long in spirit are the patient. The high in spirit are the proud. The poor in spirit are those who humbly recognize their dependence on God. They know that the only good they can hope for in their lives must come from the God who "raises the poor from the dust and lifts the needy from the ash heap" (Ps. 113:7). The *New English Bible* translates this image well: "Blessed are those who know their need of God." The poor in spirit recognize that they have nothing and are nothing in themselves. They are therefore more keenly aware of their dependence on God.

While all are in need of God, not all recognize it. Jesus' parable of the Pharisee and the tax collector (Luke 18:9-14) provides an illustration of this fact. Luke tells us that Jesus spoke this parable to those who trusted in their own righteousness, and the Pharisee in the parable exemplifies this attitude. He smugly boasted to God about all of his religious accomplishments. He could name every good deed that he had ever done and assumed that they could be cashed in with God like poker chips. Having achieved all that he thought God required, he could look down his nose at others who were less religiously accomplished. He glorified himself by comparing his own works with the failures of others. He made out the test, graded it himself, and gave himself an *A* plus.

The attitude of the tax collector was completely different. He came before God with empty hands and a broken and contrite heart. He stood afar off, did not even dare to lift up his eyes to heaven, and beat his breast because of his sense of shame. He was overwhelmed by the chasm that he thought existed between himself and God. His plea for mercy was all that he had to offer God. The Pharisee believed that he was great without God's help. The tax collector knew he was nothing without God's help. The Pharisee did not ask God for anything in his prayer because he did not think he needed anything from God. The tax collector could only cast himself on the mercy of God and was surprised to find an amazing grace that would save even a wretch like him.

Jesus affirms in this first beatitude that the more you are aware of your need for God, the more you are going to cheer the reign of God that is breaking in with Jesus' ministry of healing and teaching. Those who view their gifts from God as their own achievements are not open to God's grace. They think that they can rely on themselves. Those who know how much they need the hope of a new life are more likely to respond when it comes. And they are to be congratulated because God is acting right now to help.

Theirs is the kingdom of heaven. Matthew tells us that Jesus had been preaching "the gospel of the kingdom" throughout Galilee (4:23, RSV). In the Sermon on the Mount, Jesus announces that the kingdom is present to be entered into (5:20) and that it is to be the first priority for disciples (6:33). The phrase "kingdom of heaven" forms a kind of frame around the Sermon (5:3; 7:21). The promise, "theirs is the kingdom of heaven," also brackets the first and the eighth beatitudes (5:3, 10). The first word of good news is that God loves the lowly. So, "Stand up, you humble ones! God intends you for his kingdom."

Blessed are those who mourn (5:4)

Some readers presume that the second beatitude is intended to soothe all those who undergo the ordeals of life—the crushing failures, the bitter sorrows. Blessed are those who mourn, for they shall find solace. But this beatitude does not apply to mourners of all stripes. Not all who weep are blessed, and not all sorrow finds comfort. In this beatitude, Jesus has in mind a special kind of heartache.

Who are the happy mourners? In 2 Corinthians 7:10, Paul speaks of a godly grief and a worldly grief. The difference between the two is what causes the anguish and what are the results. Worldly distress is prompted by such personal disappointments as not getting a promotion, not having enough money, not getting your own way. Revelation 18:9-13 provides a classic example of worldly sorrow. The kings of the earth who sold out to the great Babylon and lived in the lap of luxury bemoan the smoke of her burning and cry out, "Alas!" The merchants of the earth also mourn because no one buys their cargo anymore, and their list of cargo includes slaves, human lives. Godly grief, by contrast, is inspired by such things as guilt for one's sins (see James 4:9 and 1 Cor. 5:2). It is the broken spirit of the psalmist pleading for forgiveness and renewal (Ps. 51:10, 17).

As godly grief and worldly grief differ in their cause, they also differ in their results. It is commonly said that trouble teaches us to pray. But that is not always the case. It may cause us to curse, to grow bitter, to mope, to whine, or to seek revenge. Worldly grief leads only to more woe. Godly grief, however, produces a repentance that leads to salvation (2 Cor. 7:10). It does not curse life or become resentful. It does not lead to sulking or rancor, and it alone will find comfort.

The mourners that Jesus has in mind in this beatitude are those who have a godly sorrow. They sorrow over the evil in their own lives, but they also lament the wretched state of the world. They mourn over what seems to be the eclipse of God's purpose on earth; and they cry out, "How long, O Lord?" (Rev. 6:10). When will the hatred that darkens human hearts be purged from the earth?

They shall be comforted. The good news of the coming of Jesus is that God forgives sins and that God will right every wrong. Those who mourn over their sins will be comforted in the atoning cross of Christ. Those who groan over the Satanic tyranny that seems to have a stranglehold on the world (see Rom. 8:22-23) and who ache for God's will to be done on earth will also be comforted. The time is coming when every knee shall bow and every tongue shall acknowledge that Jesus

Christ is Lord of the universe. Sin and death will be destroyed (Rev. 21:4). In Jesus, the light is already beginning to consume the darkness. And so he says, "Happy are the mourners."

Blessed are the meek (5:5)

Many of us are not too sure about this beatitude because meekness suggests something negative to us. It calls to mind softness, passivity, even cowardice. The word is associated with the milquetoast, doormat personality that almost seems to invite injury and insult. The average person today would be insulted if you were to call him or her "a meek little person." It implies that that person is weak. Our world glorifies the macho, not the meek. Meekness is something more suitable for a mouse.

Who are the meek? In the Bible, meekness is not something to be despised. It is one of the gifts of the Spirit (Gal. 5:23). But meekness is not simply an attitude of passive submission. Some might be surprised to learn that Moses is described as meek when he did not repay the slander of Miriam and Aaron but beseeched the Lord to cure Miriam from her leprosy (Num. 12:3-13). Jesus describes himself as being "meek and lowly" (Matt. 11:29, KJV; see 2 Cor. 10:1). He enters Jerusalem "gentle and riding on a donkey" (Matt. 21:5, quoting Zech. 9:9). He does not come as a warrior bent on rampage and destruction. We can learn from this that the quality Jesus has in mind is not the bowed head and the downcast eye of a beaten slave. It is the sure step and quiet determination of the royal Christ who goes to the cross. It is the attitude of the one who is able to endure suffering without bitterness or the desire to retaliate.

In the ancient world, meekness connoted power that was bridled by gentleness. That is why the ancient Greeks did not say "meek as a mouse" but "meek as a lion." It referred to controlled strength. The person who is meek does not go berserk when challenged or injured. The meek are strong, but they are not like the rough, the hard, the violent, and the angry who are so glorified in motion pictures. Perhaps the translation of the French *La Sante Bible* may change our minds about this beatitude. It translates this beatitude, Blessed are the "debonair." The style of the meek contrasts with that of the greedy go-getter. The self-assertive and self-advertising person believes that if you are to inherit the earth you must seize it by crushing all who are in your way. The meek accepts it as a gift.

They shall inherit the earth. The prophet Isaiah says that the one "who makes me his refuge will inherit the land and possess my holy mountain" (Isa. 57:13; see also 60:21). The inheritance of the earth does not come as a result of violent aggression but as a legacy, a gift. The humble pious are heirs to the king.

Blessed are those who hunger and thirst after righteousness (5:6)

Jesus applauds the hungry and the thirsty. The image of hunger and thirst would have communicated forcefully in a parched land that was frequently visited by famines. There were many who suffered from physical hunger and thirst. Food and drink are basic necessities for human survival. But humans also have spiritual needs, and only the one true God can satisfy them. In this beatitude, Jesus pronounces that those who have a gnawing spiritual hunger and thirst are blessed.

Who are the hungry and thirsty? The prophet Amos said, "The days are coming when I will send a famine through the land—not a famine of food or a thirst for water, but a famine of hearing the words of the LORD" (8:11). A famished Jesus rebuffs Satan in the wilderness by reciting the Scripture: "Man shall not live by bread alone but by every word that proceeds from the mouth of God" (Matt. 4:4, RSV; Deut. 8:3). In John's Gospel, he says, "My food is to do the will of him who sent me" (John 4:34). The hungry and thirsty that Jesus has in mind are those who are just like him; they pine to do what God requires. They have a burning desire to see God's will accomplished in their own lives and in the world.

They shall be satisfied. We live in a world where people hunger and thirst but for all the wrong things. We live in an escape-hungry society. People hunger for gourmet food and thirst for the finest wines at the trendiest restaurants. They hanker after status, recognition, admiration, money, success, and sex. But they are never satisfied. Two things have been said to characterize our affluent society: our self-indulgence and our lack of contentment.

Many feel a huge void in their lives and are ready to grab for anything that promises to fill their emptiness. What they get usually turns out to be a little more spiritual junk food. It is a lot like cotton candy. It looks so delicious and inviting; but when one takes a bite, it is nothing but air. It is neither nourishing nor filling, and one is left wanting only more. Jesus taught that there is more to life than food and clothes and material prosperity. Many people find out too late what it is that could have filled their souls with meaning. The coming of Jesus means that our deepest longings for fellowship with God can be fulfilled. Through Christ we can enter a new relationship with God and can be filled to overflowing.

Blessed are the merciful (5:7)

The people of Israel first experienced God as a God of mercy. In fact, one of the fundamental attributes of God in the Old Testament is his mercy. God is merciful, gracious, and slow to anger (Exod. 34:6; Ps. 116:5; Prov. 12:10). Time and again, God acted mercifully to deliver his people. He is also one to whom sinners can appeal for mercy. Because God is so merciful, he expects his people to be merciful as well.

Who are the merciful? Two parables in Matthew's Gospel single out mercy or the lack of it as one of the criterion that will decide one's ultimate destiny. The parable of the sheep and goats (Matt. 25:31-45) shows that mercy is an inward sentiment that leads to direct action. It is compassion that reaches out to help another. The one who is merciful responds automatically to those in need simply because they are in need.

Mercy is also compassion that spares another. The parable of the unforgiving servant (Matt. 18:21-35) makes it clear that because God has been merciful to us, we are expected to be merciful to others. In this parable, the servant of a king is unable to pay a mammoth debt. When he and his family are about to be sold into slavery to defray the loss, he pleads: "Lord, have patience with me, and I will repay you everything." In modern phraseology, he wants the chance to reschedule his payments. Is he really so foolish as to believe that he can make up this colossal debt and avoid any penalty if he only has a little more time? But the king's compassion goes far beyond the frantic appeal of his servant. The servant asked for patience. The king shows compassion. He does not let him try to raise the money within a month. He does not put him on a time payment plan. He writes off the debt entirely—something the servant never even dared to ask. It would seem that he is forgiven with no strings attached, but as the story unfolds there is an unspoken expectation.

The servant jubilantly leaves the presence of the king and happens on a fellow servant who owes him only a meager sum. The economy must have been in a tailspin because this servant is also unable to pay. He, too, begs for more time—a more reasonable request since his debt is small. But the other servant has the gall to seize this fellow by the neck and throw him into prison until he repays the last penny. When word of his heartlessness gets around, the king angrily denounces him: "Evil servant, I forgave you all that was owed by you since you appealed to me. Was it not necessary that you have mercy on your fellow servant as I had on you?"

Without the example of the king, the behavior of the servant might be understandable. With it, his action is inexcusable. The reason the king was so enraged is because he had shown such extravagant mercy on this servant and the servant responded by showing extravagant lack of pity to another. The parable drives home the point that mercy requires mercy.

Before God, we are just like the servant who owes a whopping debt and is completely penniless. Yet God has forgiven us the entire amount. If we have been on the receiving end of so much mercy, how can we still insist on getting our due from others? If we are no longer judged by God according to a balance sheet of debts and credits, how can we insist that others continue under that system in their relationships with us? The disciple who lives by God's mercy cannot withhold mercy from others.

They shall receive mercy. Everyone hopes that God will show mercy in the judgment. This desire is captured by a Scottish epitaph.

Here lie I, Martin Elginbrodde
Ha'e mercy o' my soul Lord God,
as I wad do, were I Lord God
And ye were Martin Elginbrodde.

But how can we expect mercy from God, when we show none to others? Jesus says that only the merciful can hope to receive mercy from God.

The statement that the merciful will receive mercy has nothing to do with the idea of "tit for tat." To understand this promise we may imagine mercy flowing through a kind of pipeline. When the valve of the pipeline is open, mercy flows both ways. One receives mercy and bestows it. When the valve is shut so that mercy is cut off to another, it also shuts oneself off from receiving mercy. Whatever it is in people that makes them unable to be merciful and forgiving also makes them unable to receive mercy or forgiveness. Jesus says that the fruit of forbearance with others is God's forbearance with us.

Blessed are the pure in heart (5:8)

In Jesus' culture, the heart was considered to be the control center of a person's innermost being. It shaped a person's life (Matt. 11:29). It was the place where one made decisions that determined one's attitude in life (Matt. 6:21). It was the seat of one's feelings, passions, and aspirations, and the source of one's thoughts, words, and deeds (Matt. 5:28; 9:4; 12:34). The condition of one's heart is going to determine one's relationship with God.

Who are the pure in heart? To be pure in heart may refer either to sinlessness of the heart or to singleness of heart. According to the first view, Jesus is alluding to inner purity. Those who are pure in heart have pure thoughts (5:28) and pure motives (6:1-6, 16-18). Consequently, their actions are also pure. Jesus pictures the heart as a kind of spiritual window that must be kept clear if one is going to see God. The heart that is clouded by lust or blinded by ambition is not able to focus clearly on God. Those whose hearts are unsoiled by sin are able to see clearly.

According to the second view, Jesus has in mind the person with a one-track mind when it comes to the things of God. The pure in heart are those who center their lives wholly upon God (see Matt. 22:37). For example, James tells his readers: "Come near to God and he will come near to you. Wash your hands, you sinners, and purify your hearts, you double-minded" (4:8). For James, the double-minded person is religiously split in two. He tries to do the impossible, to follow two separate paths at the same time. The ones who have cleansed their hearts, however, are those who are completely focused only on God.

They shall see God. Jesus promised that the pure in heart will see God. To "see God" does not mean that they will have their curiosity satisfied about what God looks like but that they will come into God's presence. "To see the face of someone" was a Palestinian idiom meaning that one was given an audience with someone of consequence (compare Gen. 43:3, 5; 2 Sam. 14:24). For example, one was said to come before the face of God during the temple worship. The psalmist says, "My soul thirsts for God, for the living God. When shall I come and behold the face of God?" (Ps. 42:2, RSV). In Revelation 22:3-4, John sees the throne of God and of the Lamb and says that his servants shall worship him and shall see his face. The statement means that they dwell in the presence of God.

T. W. Manson points out that ritual defilements and bodily impurities of various kinds barred one from coming into God's presence during temple worship. Outward ritual purity was believed to be as vital as inward purity. But Jesus says that fellowship with God depends *only* on a heart that loves goodness with single-minded devotion and that hates evil.[3] That is what truly counts with God. No one with a pure heart will be banished from the presence of God.

Blessed are the peacemakers (5:9)

A teenage tennis star was asked why she was wearing an earring with a peace sign. She responded: "It's not political. It's the 'in' thing. I want peace. It's cool." Everybody wants peace; it's the "in" thing. But what do people mean when they talk about peace? The peace that Jesus has in mind has nothing to do with peace of mind and refers to something more than the absence of war. While many may think that peace is "cool," how far are they willing to go to make peace? We should note that Jesus does not say blessed are the peacelovers but the peacemakers. In Luke 19:41 Jesus laments over the city of Jerusalem, saying: "If you . . . had only known on this day what would bring you peace . . ." In the beatitudes, he pronounces blessed those who not only know the things that make for peace but who take action to make peace.

Who are the peacemakers? Peacemaking is something that is active and persistent. The peacemaker energetically strives to make peace. The peacemaker resolves conflict, restores relationships, repairs broken bonds, and respects the rights of others. The peacemaker aims at bringing harmony to two squabbling parties (see Phil. 4:2-3). Peacemakers do more than wear earrings with peace signs. They are ready to leave the altar in the middle of a sacrifice to seek reconciliation with a brother who has something against them (Matt. 5:23-24). They are prepared to go to a fellow Christian when they have something against him, that is, when he has sinned against them (Matt. 18:15). They are not out to convict the other person but to convince him of the need to repent and thereby restore peace. Their primary concern is to do something to help the sinner so that they can mend the breach and gain a brother.

Peacemakers not only resist the urge to retaliate (Matt. 5:39), they weed out the deadly plants of violence that can take root like weeds in the lives of people. They love their enemies and pray for them (Matt. 5:44). Peacemakers are also prepared to go to those who hate them with a message of God's love simply because they are the followers of the Prince of Peace who did the same thing.

They shall be called sons of God. Jesus says that peacemakers shall be hailed as sons of God. The phrase "son of" reflects another Palestinian idiom. It is based on the belief that a person's actions betray his or her origins. Those who duplicate or express in their own way of life that of another are called "the sons of" the one they imitate. For example, Jesus condemns his opponents as "the sons of those who murdered the prophets" (Matt. 23:31, RSV). He does not mean that their fathers and grandfathers once killed prophets. He means that they display the very same spirit as those earlier assassins who oppressed the righteous (see also the expression "sons of" in Matt. 5:45; 13:38).

Peacemakers are "sons of God" in the sense that they share in what God is doing in our world. God is the author of peace, and peacemakers are imitators of God. God has disarmed the chaos of sin in the world by giving his own Son. As Jesus plunged into the midst of human life to bring order out of ruin, reconciliation out of estrangement, and love in the place of hate, so does the peacemaker.

Blessed are those who are persecuted for righteousness' sake (5:10-12)

It is puzzling to think of the persecuted as somehow blessed. We would put them in the category of the unfortunate. But the New Testament has a surprisingly positive attitude toward persecution. It is a reminder of divine favor.

Who are the persecuted? Many people in our world are persecuted for a variety of reasons. It should be made clear that the persecution Jesus is talking about is brought on by one's devotion to Christ. It is the result of disciples living up to and living out their calling. We can see many examples in the New Testament of Christians being abused for their faith. The Sanhedrin tried to bully the apostles to stop them from preaching about the resurrection in Jerusalem. They discovered, however, that they could shut the apostles up in prison, but they could not make them shut up. And the Christians' response to this oppression was to rejoice that they were counted worthy to suffer for the name of Christ (Acts 5:41). In Acts 8:1, Luke tells us that a great persecution came upon the church in Jerusalem. Christians were imprisoned or driven out of town. We would expect the persecution to cool zeal, to drain faithfulness, and to weaken loyalty. We might expect Acts 8:4 to read: violent persecution arose against the church; therefore, those who were oppressed all lay low until the storm blew over. Instead, Luke writes, *therefore* the Christians kept right on doing the very same thing that brought on the persecution; they continued to preach the gospel. The early Christians were what Paul calls fools for Christ (1 Cor. 4:10). After every beating, they got up again to preach the same things that got them the beating. Or, if they were not able to get up again, some other fools for Christ showed up to take their place.

A satirist from the second century by the name of Lucian held Christians in contempt. In his *The Passing of Peregrinus 13*, he writes about the arrest of Christians: "The poor wretches have convinced themselves, first and foremost, that they are going to be immortal and live for all time, in consequence of which they despise death and even willingly give themselves into custody, most of them." Even in trying to defame Christians, Lucian testifies to their great courage in the face of death.

People have been persecuted for Christ throughout history. Will Campbell wrote of a woman who in 1573 prayed fervently for her children.[4] Her name was Maeyken Wens. She was an Anabaptist who lived in Antwerp. She had been arrested a few days earlier for proclaiming the gospel of Christ as she understood it from her personal reading of the Scripture and from study and discussion with others of like faith. She weathered a trial for heresy and endured bodily torture and did not buckle under the pressure of the clerics and civil authorities. After six months, she would not promise to stop preaching the Word as she understood it from her own reading of the Bible. So the authorities did what they thought they had to do; they sentenced her to death. Included in her sentence was the stipulation that her tongue be screwed fast to the roof of her mouth so that she might not testify along the way as they took her to the stake where she was to be burned.

That day her teenage son, Adriaen, took his youngest brother, three-year-old Hans Mattheus, and they stood near the stake so that her first and last children might be near her at her moment of death. Three other women and a man were to die that day for the same terrible offense—preaching the gospel unauthorized. When the flames were lit, Adriaen fainted. He could not witness the horror. But when it was all over and the ashes had cooled, he sifted through them until he found the screw that had silenced his mother's tongue. When we read of the great sacrifices of so many for their faith, we do well to recall the words penned by Isaac Watts:

Must I be carried to the skies
on flowery beds of ease
while others fought to win the prize
and sailed through bloody seas?

Peter wrote to encourage fellow Christians who were beseiged by foes:

> Dear friends, do not be surprised at the painful trial you are suffering, as though something strange were happening to you. But rejoice that you participate in the sufferings of Christ, so that you may be overjoyed when his glory is revealed. If you are insulted because of the name of Christ, you are blessed, for the Spirit of glory and of God rests on you. *1 Peter 4:12-14*

Reasons for rejoicing. When persecution for our faith comes our way, we are not to become embittered but to rejoice. Jesus offers two reasons for doing so. First, those who are persecuted and reviled are the heirs to the kingdom of God. As Paul knew, the sufferings of this present evil age do not even begin to compare with the glory that is to be revealed (Rom. 8:18). Second, the persecuted are in good company. They join the long lines of God's prophets who were hounded by those who rejected their message. Great is their reward in heaven.

The Influence of Kingdom Citizens (5:13-16)

The salt of the earth (5:13)

It is hard to know precisely what Jesus had in mind when he told his disciples that they were the salt of the earth because salt had a variety of functions in the ancient world. It was used as a condiment, a preservative, a fire catalyst, a fertilizer, an antiseptic, and, in Judaism, was associated with the covenant in sacrifices. What does it mean to be the salt of the earth?

Jesus may have thought of salt's widespread use as a seasoning. Job asked, "Is tasteless food eaten without salt? Or is there flavor in the white of an egg?" (Job 6:6). As a little child once said, "Salt is what makes food taste bad when it is not on it." Jesus may be saying that the disciples are the characteristic tang that brings out the quality in the world.

Since there was no means of refrigeration, salt was vital as a preservative. One of the most distinguished towns of eastern Galilee was Taricheae. The name means "saltings" and was derived from the salted fish industry there. Jesus may be picturing the disciples as salt that fights off spiritual decay in the world.

Salt was also used as an antiseptic. You can imagine how it stung when it was used to treat an open wound. It is significant that Jesus calls his disciples the salt and not the sugar of the earth. Salt has a bite to it. But it is necessary to fight the rot and rid the world of the infection of sin. If this is the image that Jesus has in mind, the disciples, as salt, are not to soothe the guilt of humankind or to sweeten their prospects for the judgment. Jesus' commands allow for no compromise. The disciples are to challenge sharply the world and its sin.

Salt also served as a fire catalyst. An outdoor Palestinian oven was called "earth" (see Ps. 12:6; Job 28:5), and the people frequently used dried dung as fuel. To make the ovens burn better, the bottom of the kiln was lined with flat plates of salt, and the dung was also sprinkled with a little salt. As a chemical agent, salt accelerated and improved the burning. Over time, however, the heat caused the salt plates to change chemically in such a way that it impeded the burning process. Then the salt had to be discarded. This fact fits the parallel saying in Luke 14:34-35 that salt which has lost its saltiness is fit neither for the earth (the kiln) nor for the dung hill (to prepare the fuel). If this is what Jesus visualizes, then the disciples are to be a catalyst that helps ignite and sustain spiritual fires on the earth.

Salt was also used widely as a fertilizer. It killed weeds and, in proper amounts, improved the soil. As salt, the disciples are to improve the soil so that it might be more receptive to the seed of God's Word (see Matt. 13:3-9, 18-23).

Salt was also associated with the covenant and sacrifice in Judaism. We read in Leviticus 2:13, "Season all your grain offerings with salt. Do not leave the salt of the covenant of your God out of your grain offerings; add salt to all your offerings" (see Num. 18:19). The saying about salt immediately follows the beatitude for those who are persecuted and reviled, and it may continue the idea of suffering and sacrifice. Salt is only useful when it gives of itself. As salt, the disciples are to sacrifice themselves for the world to save others from the wrath of God's judgment.

Jesus may have had in mind any one or all of these images when he uttered this saying. One thing is clear: the statement

"You are the salt of the earth," is a word of assurance. The emphasis is on the "you are"!

But it may also be taken as a word of warning. Pure sodium chloride (NaCl) does not change its chemical properties. But the salt that was mined from the area around the Dead Sea could have impurities, and the pure salt might leach out, leaving a bitter residue. If salt "becomes foolish" (the literal meaning of the word in Greek), it is good for nothing. It is simply discarded. Savorless Christianity is as absurd and as despised as saltless salt. If Christians lose their peculiar tang, their purification or catalytic qualities, their capacity to enhance the yield of the soil, or their willingness to spend themselves for others, then the world is the worse off. But the saltless salt will be dumped.

The light of the world (5:14-16)

Jesus continues his affirmation of the disciples by telling them that they are the light of the world. If they are light, they are going to be visible, like a city set on a hill. A city on the hill makes a strong impression. Its lights brighten the whole horizon at night, and all who pass by cannot help but see it. Jesus expands this notion by saying that no one lights a lamp only to douse it promptly by putting it under a bushel basket. It is not that people *should* not hide their light under baskets, but that they *do* not do this. The point is that God does not do such things either. God does not provide a lamp to enlighten the world and then immediately snuff it out. God sends light into the world to shine.

Moses reminded the people of Israel that they were God's special possession (Deut. 26:18-19). They were to keep God's commandments, and God would raise them high above all the nations. They were to be a people holy to God. Their vocation was to bring praise, fame, and glory to God. Isaiah proclaimed that Israel was to be a light to the nations, a beacon that would draw those in darkness to God and to God's city set on Mount Zion (Isa. 2:2-3; 42:6-7; 49:6). But there were some in Israel who mistook responsibility for special privilege. They shone only for themselves. Their scribes hid the lamp of God (Ps. 119:105) so that it did not give light to anyone (Matt. 15:14; 23:13). Those who were confident that they were a guide to the blind and a light to those in darkness (Rom. 2:19) turned out to be blind guides entombed in their own darkness (Matt. 23:16).

Jesus says that it is his disciples who are now the light of the world (see Phil. 2:15). They are the new community of Zion set on a hill that will draw people to God. And Jesus intends for them to radiate the truth. "Let your light shine" in the English translation is the only way to render the third person imperative in the Greek. But this translation unfortunately implies that we are only to allow our light to shine. In the Greek, it is a command to shine the light. Jesus says, you are the light of the world, so shine!

The doing of good works (5:15-16)

Jesus expects his disciples to make an impression on the earth as salt, on the world as light, and upon humanity as doers of good works. But the disciples of Jesus are not immune to temptations. A number of things may lead the disciples to be less than what they truly are.

In times of persecution (5:12), the disciples may be tempted to hide their lights. They may want to lay low instead of standing tall. They may want to go into hiding instead of going public. They may be afraid that if they are seen by people they will be trampled. But light, if it is light, shines. If it does not shine, it is not light but darkness. And Jesus warns that if they fail to be what they are, they will be thrown out and trampled anyway.

Disciples may also be tempted to retreat from the world. But salt, if it is to do anything, must come into direct contact with the substance we want it to effect. It does not work from a distance. If it is to retard corruption, start a fire, or whatever, it must *touch*.

One of the ways that the disciples shine their light is through their good works. They may be tempted to become showy in their display of piety (see Matt. 6:1-6, 16-18). They may want to dazzle others with their good works so that *they* are glorified, not God. Both salt and light function best when they are least visible. You know when they are absent. But if you see a pile of salt on your food, it means that there is too much. If you are blinded by a lamp, you are not able to read. Jesus makes it clear that our good works should not direct attention back to us but to the Father in heaven. The purpose of shining our light is to point others to the God who is working in us.

A tiny group of disciples might be tempted to despair of having any significant effect on the world, let alone their own community. After all, who are the poor, the mourners, the meek, the hungering, and the persecuted when compared to the entire world? They are nobodies. How few they seem and how powerless. But salt and light can have great effect in small quantities—a pinch of salt does wonders for food; a tiny flashlight floods a dark cavern with light. Likewise, each disciple's life has immeasurable potential—and how the world was changed by God working in and through just a handful of them!

Questions for Further Reflection

1. What is a beatitude?

2. What is attractive about the blessings promised in the beatitudes?

3. What do the symbols "salt" and "light" suggest about our role in the church and society?

➠ Action Step

Make a list of the beatitudes and the promises contained in each saying. Identify one present-day application for your life from each beatitude.

3

THE RIGHTEOUSNESS OF KINGDOM CITIZENS

Matthew 5:17-48

Jesus begins his instructions on life under God's reign with a key statement about his relationship to the Law and the prophets. He cautions his listeners not to presume that he came to do away with the Law or the prophets. The fact that Jesus boldly declares six times, "You have heard it said . . . but I say to you," might have led some to think that Jesus was undermining the Law with his teaching. Did Jesus dare to swap his own words for important provisions in the Law? But Jesus assures his listeners beforehand that he does not abolish or invalidate the Law of Moses. The Law and the prophets faithfully express God's will. What Jesus does and teaches complies with them; but more, he completes them.

The Fulfillment of the Law (5:17-19)

Jesus fulfills the Law and the prophets in three ways: by living in perfect obedience to them, by recapturing their divine purpose, and by completing their promises. He embodies God's demand that his people be a holy people. For this reason, the disciples are to listen to him and not to the other voices that claim to have authority from on high.

Jesus lived in perfect obedience to the Law and the prophets (5:17)

Jesus faithfully kept the Law. He submitted to John's baptism in order to "fulfill all righteousness" (Matt. 3:15). In the temptation, Jesus faced down the enemy that haunts all of us. Satan tried to preempt the Spirit and direct Jesus' life. Satan vied with God's will with lying words that sounded religious, but Jesus successfully countered each temptation with God's Word (Matt. 4:4, 7, 10). He parried the credo of practical necessity, "You have to eat; your physical needs must be met," with the command that obedience to the Word of God comes first (4:3-4). He resisted the word of pride and special privilege that says, "You are someone favored by God; test God out to see if he will live up to his promises." He would not put God to the test (4:5-7). He combated the word of selfish ambition that chases after worldly power and glory. The devil claimed that the world was his to do with as he pleased (see 1 John 5:19), and he offered it all to Jesus on easy terms. He would give it to him. No need to follow the hard road of obedience that would lead from Gethsemane to Golgotha. Jesus banished Satan by his uncompromising obedience to God (4:8-10). The gospel story shows that Jesus was perfectly obedient to God's will each step of the way.

By contrast, the rival Jewish teachers are shown in Matthew's Gospel to be corrupt. Because of their wickedness, they are quite unreliable as guides to the true meaning of God's Law. Jesus calls them sons of snakes who draw from an evil treasure and who cannot give voice to anything good (12:33-37). They are hypocrites who wish to bask in the admiration of others (23:5). Like whitewashed tombs, their outer appearance masks the stench and decay within (23:27-28). They are blind guides who will lead everyone who follows them into the pit (15:14). Who is it that one should heed, those false teachers who put on a show of piety or the one who sincerely performs what God requires in the Law?

Jesus recaptured the purpose of the Law and the prophets (5:18)

Jesus was not only the perfect expression of what God intended in the Law, he gave perfect expression to what God's Law required. He reclaimed the original intention of the Law and the prophets. In setting forth God's intention in the Law, Jesus did not set aside the Law.

When Jesus presented what we call "the Golden Rule," he stressed that "this sums up the Law and the prophets" (7:12). What he taught was not contrary to the Law and the prophets; it was what they were all about. They still needed to be obeyed then, and they need to be obeyed today—but as interpreted by Jesus, because he intensified their demand.

The purpose of the Law was to lead one to God and to point the way to a godly life. But the rival Jewish teachers had littered the pathway with manmade barriers that distracted people from what was vital. Some of their rules even hampered obedience. Jesus blamed these teachers for misleading the people. Their traditions, which Jesus labeled "the traditions of men," could be manipulated to dodge basic human duties. Their legal opinions made it possible, for example, to sidestep God's commandment to honor one's parents (Matt. 15:1-9).

Jesus also accused the Jewish teachers of saddling the people with heavy burdens that had nothing to do with God's purposes (Matt. 23:4). The heap of regulations regarding such things as ritual purity and the proper observance of the Sabbath bewildered most people. Worse, it missed the whole point. Jesus indicted the scribes and Pharisees for "majoring on the minors while minoring on the majors." They insisted on tithing herbs such as mint, dill, and cummin that were not even mentioned in the Law, while neglecting such crucial matters as justice, mercy, and faith (Matt. 23:23). When it came to the requirement of mercy, the Jewish teachers completely flopped (Matt. 9:9-13; 12:1-8). Their strict attention to trivia blinded them to God's will. They strained out gnats and swallowed camels whole. But their greatest guilt was shutting the way into the kingdom. Like spoilsports, they refused to enter the kingdom themselves and blocked the door for others (Matt. 23:13).

Jesus' teaching redirected the way that Scriptures are to be read. He ascended the mountain as a kind of new Moses who gives the definitive interpretation of the Law. He cleared away much of the manmade rubble that surrounded the observance of the Law. To give one example, Jesus sweeps away all the claptrap concerning valid and invalid oaths by saying that God's intention is for people to be truthful and for a "yes" to mean a "yes" (5:37). Honesty does not need an oath to prop it up.

The characteristic of the scribes' and Pharisees' interpretation of the Law was their meticulous attention to matters of external ritual purity. The distinctive characteristic of Jesus' interpretation of the Law is his insistence that the love of God and the love of neighbor are foremost. When Jesus is asked later in the story, "Which is the greatest commandment in the Law?" his answer is, "To love the Lord your God with all your heart, soul, and mind." He then mentions a second, "To love your neighbor as yourself." He explains that the whole Law and the prophets hang on these two commandments (Matt. 22:34-40). These two commands are the linchpin of God's Law. And Jesus' teaching restores them to supreme importance as the sum and substance of the Law and the prophets.

Jesus fulfilled the promise of the Law and the prophets (5:19)

Jesus fulfilled the Law and the prophets in a third and even more significant way. The words, "I have come," express Jesus' awareness that he had a special status and that he came with a special mission.

His statement affirmed that the Scriptures witnessed to him. The Law and the prophets, as God's revelation to humanity, especially had to do with the coming of Jesus. Moses prophesied that God would speak anew through a prophet like himself (Deut. 18:15-20). Jesus was that promised prophet who gave the true interpretation of God's Law. To this point in the story, Matthew has gone out of his way to tell his reader that events in Jesus' life fulfilled the Scriptures (Matt. 1:22-23; 2:6, 15, 18, 23; 3:3; 4:14-16). Their complete veracity is therefore confirmed by his arrival.

Jesus fulfilled the long-awaited promise of the Scriptures. But fulfillment also implies transcendence. When Jesus appeared as God with us (Matt. 1:23), the center of gravity shifted to him. The six statements that follow in 5:21-48 make it clear that Jesus is the norm by which the teaching of the Law and the prophets must be evaluated. The Law and the prophets remain valid, but Jesus is the yardstick by which to gauge our obedience to the rulings of Scripture. He is the interpretive guide who unlocks their true meaning. He is the authority by which the authority of Scripture is established. Such things as Sabbath regulations (Matt. 12:1-14), food laws (Matt. 15:1-20), and temple sacrifices (Matt. 17:24-27) have been transcended by Christ's life, teaching, and death and resurrection. Jesus is the Lord of the Sabbath and of the temple.

Christ is the fulfillment of the Law and the prophets; but, as the Son of God, he now has the same status as the Law and the prophets. Four passages in Matthew reveal the unique status of Jesus' words. The Sermon on the Mount concludes with the warning that the one who is wise hears Jesus' words and does them. The one who is foolish ignores them (Matt. 7:24-27). Obedience to Jesus' words will determine one's ultimate future. Three of the disciples witness the transfiguration of Jesus in the presence of Moses and Elijah. But then Moses and Elijah vanish; and the voice from the cloud proclaims, "This is my beloved Son, with whom I am well pleased; listen to him" (Matt. 17:5, RSV). In 5:18, Jesus tells us that not even the smallest detail of the Law will pass away until heaven and earth pass away. But in 24:35 he says that heaven and earth will pass away but his words will not; his words are eternal. At the conclusion of the Gospel of Matthew, Jesus instructs his disciples to go into the world to make disciples and to teach them to keep all the things that he has taught them (Matt. 28:20). It should be clear from these passages that Jesus' words represent the ultimate expression of God's will. He truly fulfills the Law and the prophets.

The Higher Righteousness (5:20)

Jesus must have startled his listeners when he went on to announce, "Unless your righteousness exceeds that of the scribes and Pharisees, you will not enter into the kingdom of heaven." No one would ever question that the righteousness of those who wanted to enter into the kingdom of heaven must exceed that of the tax collector or the heathen. But Jesus insists that the disciples' righteousness must also exceed that of the proverbially righteous. Although Jesus assails the righteousness of the scribes and Pharisees as hypocrisy, most people in his day regarded them as exceptionally devout. Few others went to such extremes to be pious. Paul testifies to that devotion when he recounts his former life as a Pharisee. He tells the Galatians that he outstripped all of his contemporaries in his zeal for the traditions of the fathers (Gal. 1:14). He tells the Philippians that when it came to righteousness based on obedience to the Law he was blameless (Phil. 3:5-6). But Jesus rates the righteousness of the scribes and Pharisees as totally inadequate for entry into the kingdom of heaven. And after Paul encountered the risen Lord on the road to Damascus, he came to realize this fact, too. All of his proud religious achievements were as filthy rags, rubbish (Phil. 3:8). He recognized that one could be ruled by a rule book but still not be ruled by God. God insists on something greater.

This concern for a greater righteousness captures the main theme of what follows. The issue is: What are you doing that is more than others (5:47)? The "more" that Jesus requires has to do with both quantity and quality. It also makes clear that the righteousness Jesus has in mind in the Sermon on the Mount has to do with conduct. What follows in 5:21-48 is a norm of conduct that sets the disciples apart from others in their attitudes, in their words, and in their actions.

This section of the Sermon on the Mount (5:21-48) is frequently called the "antitheses." The verses highlight some of the ways that our righteousness is to outstrip the general opinion of what is required (see also 18:3). Jesus does not offer them as something optional for extra credit. They are the basic requirements of righteousness. They are examples of how Jesus interprets the Law and the prophets to reveal the will of God. The love command is the controlling principle. Our everyday relations with others are to be governed by love.

Examples of the Higher Righteousness (5:21-48)

Anger (5:21-26)

Most of us may feel quite pure and blameless when it comes to the sixth commandment, "Thou shalt not kill" (Exod. 20:13; Deut. 5:17). We are not blackhearted murderers. But Jesus shakes us from our self-righteous satisfaction throughout the

Sermon on the Mount. Here he says that even if one has never actually murdered another, one may still not be off the hook. Anyone who is *angry* with his brother shall be liable to judgment.

Moses said that the murderer will be judged (Exod. 21:12; Lev. 24:17; Num. 35:12; Deut. 17:8-13). Jesus says that the angry person will be judged. With these words, Jesus addresses those of us who may only have "looked daggers" at others, wishing them in the grave. He says that we are no less guilty than the one who actually runs another through with a knife. The elder, John, expresses the same idea: "Anyone who hates his brother is a murderer, and you know that no murderer has eternal life in him" (1 John 3:15).

We learn from this first saying that Jesus requires radical obedience to the Law. Outward compliance to the rules is not enough. True obedience must arise from the nucleus of our being. While human courts may judge the overt act (Deut. 16:18), God will judge the inner attitude (1 Sam. 16:7). If one does the deed in one's heart, one is just as blameworthy as if one had literally pulled the trigger.

Some may think it extreme to equate anger with murder. Why did Jesus do this? He is not trying to add to our list of sins for which we will be judged. What he is doing is training his sights on the root cause of murder—the angry heart. Many passages in the Old Testament address the issue of how to *punish* someone guilty of a violent act (Gen. 9:6; Exod. 21:12-14; Lev. 24:17; Num. 35:16-21); Jesus addresses the issue of how to *prevent* the violent act. If one takes care of the anger, one will eliminate the problem of murder.

Many Christians wince when they hear that Jesus likens anger to murder. They become worried that their feelings of anger are as wicked as murder. They then may think that it is unchristian ever to get angry. As a result, Christians sometimes try to cover up their anger. When they get mad, they deny it. Or they may try to camouflage their anger by expressing it in more subtle but just as deadly ways.

The danger for Christians is not that they might become angry. If we are human and not vegetables, we will get angry. The use of the present tense of the verb in the Greek, "everyone who is angry," may be translated with the sense of continuous action: "everyone who is continuously angry with his brother." The NEB translates the verb: "everyone who nurses anger in his heart." Anger is not the sin. It is a natural human reaction. The problem is how we handle the anger. Anger becomes dangerous when it is nurtured, justified, and encouraged. The Bible therefore warns us to simmer down by sundown (see Eph. 4:26, 31; Col. 3:8; 1 Tim. 2:8; James 1:19-20) because anger can eat away at the soul like a cancer. It will destroy relationships and rob our lives of joy.

Unfortunately, anger is frequently mishandled. Sometimes, instead of expressing our anger directly and appropriately, we engage in cold-war tactics and refuse to talk about the issues. Or we employ hit-and-run guerrilla warfare. We take pot shots at another in public, and that person does not know where the fire is coming from or why. The greatest danger is when the anger is allowed to well up inside until it explodes. We can find many examples in the Bible where unchecked anger resulted in homicide. Cain seethed within when his brother's sacrifice was accepted and his was not. God did not condemn him for being angry but cautioned him that sin was crouching at the door just waiting for a chance to worm its way into his life. His anger needed to be resolved. But Cain ignored the divine warning. He stoked the embers of his wrath until they burst into a blazing rage that consumed his brother (Gen. 4:3-7). Jesus commands us to do all in our power to defuse our anger before it blows up and destroys ourselves as well as others.

After this opening statement about anger, Jesus offers one example of how anger is expressed improperly—namecalling—and then gives two examples of what to do when anger comes between two people. The primary concern about namecalling is not just that it is an improper way to vent one's own anger but that it triggers anger in others. How do we feel when someone calls us names? Jesus says we are not to cause anger in others. But the next illustrations provide examples of what to do when another has become angry with us. Jesus says that we are to become peacemakers. We are to do all in our power to remove that anger and to bring about reconciliation.

Namecalling. If a person publicly insulted another individual in Jesus' culture, he or she could be dragged before the village magistrates. But Jesus says that action will also get you a court appearance before God. Demeaning others, Jesus warns, will lead to judgment. We all know the playground cliche, "Sticks and stones may break my bones, but names will never hurt me."

We also all know that it is a lie. Nothing can cut us to the quick faster than words. The problem of namecalling was far more serious in Jesus' society than ours. Most people had little to trade with except their honor, and to belittle other persons publicly was a serious matter. The victims would lose their honor and "die" in public. Jesus seems to say that when you treat persons as nothing by calling them names, you have, in effect, already murdered them. Character assassination is just another type of murder.

Jesus specifies two terms of abuse that will meet with different penalties: *Raca,* which perhaps means something like numskull, and *fool,* used in Jewish terminology in referring to an infidel or unbeliever. Labeling someone an ignoramus scorns his intelligence. Calling someone *you fool!* expresses a religious judgment of a person. It was a term used by Jews for the godless (see Ps. 14; 53; *The Book of Sirach* 22:11-12; Luke 12:20). To call someone a fool is to dispatch him to hellfire. But to do so is to infringe on God's authority. Who are we to pronounce judgment on others? We are neither omniscient nor infallible. God is the one who makes the final judgment. Jesus says that defaming another as a creedless fool will ultimately land the detractor in hellfire.

Words do matter, and Jesus warns that we will be judged for every careless word (Matt. 12:36). How much more will we be judged for those words uttered with malicious aforethought? The danger with words is that when one loses the hesitation to speak something, one begins to lose the hesitation to do it. If we describe our enemies as subhuman or evil in some way, it makes it easier to justify doing away with them. When we characterize our enemies as devils, we can rationalize doing whatever we want to eliminate them, no matter how devilish our action might be.

Sacrifice at the altar. Jesus does not picture disciples as living in a Utopian society. He is fully aware that relationships among even disciples may sour. Sometimes it is our fault, sometimes not. Our task is not to establish who is to blame but to cool the hot blood before it boils over.

Jesus offers a striking example of one way to short-circuit anger. He pictures someone at the point of offering a sacrifice to God at the altar who remembers that his brother "has something against him." This phrase implies that the one at the altar was somehow at fault.

The altar is the place where one goes to become reconciled to God. But how can one seek reconciliation with God and remain unreconciled with others? Jesus advises that one should drop everything at once and go make things right with the person who is out of sorts. Then one can return to take care of the business of sacrifice to God. This illustration implies that one approaches God through one's neighbor, and reconciliation with the neighbor outweighs even religious observances (see Matt. 9:13 and 12:7, where Jesus cites Hosea 6:6, "I desire mercy, not sacrifice"). Religious rituals are worthless if we remain at loggerheads with a brother or sister. We may stiff-arm people out of the way to score a touchdown in a football game, but we cannot stiff-arm our way to God's altar. A heart full of bitterness toward a neighbor cannot be full of love toward God. A heart that is insensitive to the hurts of others cannot expect God to lend a sympathetic ear to its hurts.

Jesus uses hyperbole to make this point. His counsel on stopping in the middle of a sacrifice would have been absolutely unthinkable. The folks Jesus was talking to lived far away from the temple in Jerusalem. If they went to the trouble and expense of making the long trip to Jerusalem, purifying themselves, and purchasing a sacrificial victim, was it reasonable to expect them to stop suddenly in midsacrifice, trek all the way back to Galilee, appease the brother, and then return to the temple to pick up the ceremony where they left off?

How approving would we be if our pastor stopped in midsermon and asked us to wait patiently while he went across town to settle things with someone he had words with yesterday? We would probably insist on first things first. Finish the sermon; and then take care of your personal issues! But Jesus' point is that first things must come first. The first thing is to do our best to defuse an explosive situation with a brother or sister, then we can take care of our worship of God.

The second image pictures a person being dragged to a hearing by an adversary. Jesus advises that we do all in our power to reconcile with this person while we are on the way before we get the book thrown at us. We should be mindful that we are going to stand before the great Judge on the final day. We would do well to settle our earthly feuds now before they come back to haunt us in the Judgment.

Adultery (5:27-30)

Marriage is something that creates a sacred link between husband and wife (Exod. 20:14; Deut. 5:18). Adultery was considered to be a great violation of that sacred bond. In the

Old Testament, adultery is defined as carnal intercourse between a man and a woman married or betrothed to another Israelite (Lev. 20:10; Deut. 22:22-27). A man did not violate his own marriage or commit adultery against his own wife by having relations with another man's wife; he violated the marriage of the woman's husband. Adultery was a sin against the neighbor.

Many assumed that unconditional fidelity was demanded only of the woman in a marriage. The incident with Tamar and Judah recorded in Genesis 38:24-26 vividly illustrates this attitude. Judah considered himself above reproach when he dallied with someone he thought to be a prostitute at his shepherds' convention, but he was ready to stone Tamar when she turned up pregnant. This chauvinistic attitude was prevalent in the Roman world. Cato said: "If you take your wife in adultery you may freely kill her without a trial. But if you commit adultery, or if another commits adultery with you, she has no right to raise a finger against you."[1]

Jesus has a totally different view of adultery. Many presume that a person is not guilty until he or she commits the physical act. Jesus says that whoever looks at a woman with lust in his heart is guilty. This statement basically redefines adultery. It is not limited to the physical act. It includes the look. Once again, Jesus' teaching makes clear that outward obedience is not enough. A person might harbor lust and consider himself righteous simply because he has refrained from following through. But that may only mean that the opportunity has never presented itself for him to fulfill his lust. Again, Jesus goes to the heart of the matter. Adultery does not just happen; it begins in the lustful heart.

We should note that Jesus directs his teaching on adultery to men, and he does not mean only the married man. It is *any* man looking at *any* woman with lust. The reason is that the laws about adultery were primarily applied to women. Males escaped punishment. Remember the story of the woman who was caught in adultery and was being taken to be stoned for her crime (John 7:53–8:11). Where was the man? He was surely no less guilty. In this teaching, Jesus takes on the double standard regarding sexual sins. He denies the right of the man to sexual license and does so on the basis that the woman, whether she is someone's wife or not, is a person who possesses the same dignity as the man. Adulterous looks are sins against her, not just her husband.

Many other religious teachers in Jesus' day also cautioned against the lustful look. Women were viewed as known occasions of sin and therefore were judged to be dangerous to the devout man. They were blamed as the cause of man's sinful passion. A story in the Babylonian Talmud illustrates this negative attitude toward women. A particularly harsh rabbi caught a man boring a hole in a fence to look at his beautiful daughter. He said to the man, "What is the meaning of this?" The man answered: "Master, if I am not worthy enough to marry her, may I not at least be worthy to catch a glimpse of her?" Therefore, he exclaimed: "My daughter, you are a source of trouble to mankind; return to the dust so that men may not sin because of you."[2] Here is a classic case of blaming the victim.

Because women were considered dangerous since they caused men to lust, many teachers prescribed the following: avoid women completely, seclude them to make it easier to avoid them, and cover them up just in case one could not avoid them. This kind of attitude was shared by some of the early church fathers. Tertullian wrote in the second century that even natural beauty ought to be obliterated by concealment and neglect, since it is dangerous to those who look at it.[3] The assumption is that men's lust is unmanageable and that the problem resides with women who are the occasion of man's lust.

Jesus approaches things quite differently. He holds us responsible for our reactions to others. He therefore does not warn his disciples about women but about themselves! He does not say do not look, but do not look with lust. The problem resides with the one who looks, not the one who is looked at. The solution is not to sequester women but to cleanse the heart of the looker. It requires rigorous discipline so that the look does not turn into a leer.

Sexual attraction is a part of being human, and Jesus does not condemn us for being sexually attracted to the opposite sex. Jesus' teaching on the look may be similar to his teaching on anger. The present tense of the verb in the phrase, "any one who looks at a woman," may suggest nursing the lustful look. There is no sin in sexual attraction. The problem is that attraction can quickly degenerate into lust.

The Greek idiom more readily expresses the problem that Jesus was trying to correct. In Greek, the verbs "to lust" and "to commit adultery" take a direct object. Our English idiom requires that we say "commits adultery with her"; such a translation implies that the woman is somehow involved. In Greek, it is more exact: the man "lusts her" and "adulterates her." Now the problem becomes clearer. The woman is dehumanized by the lustful look. She is made into an object. Lust is completely self-centered, interested only in sexual gratification. It treats other persons as things to be exploited. It adulterates them. When the lust is sated, the object of the lust is discarded (see 2 Sam. 13:1-22) and another object is sought out.

Jesus warns us to purge our hearts so that we are able to look at a person of the opposite sex and see a person, not an object. Again, Jesus uses hyperbole to drive home his point. Jesus does not expect us literally to pluck out an offending eye or to cut off an offending hand. But sin is serious business. We are to perform radical surgery on anything that would cause us to be cut off from eternal life. Unfortunately, we live in a culture that uses sex to sell everything from toothpaste to hardware. Is it any wonder that a recent study discloses that a third of married Americans have been unfaithful? And that figure does not include the many unmarried people who have multiple partners. Disciples are to cut themselves off from these kinds of influences that foster lust instead of love.

Divorce (5:31-32)

The divorce statistics in our country continue to skyrocket, and the issue is constantly before us. But when we think of divorce, we think in terms of a judgment decided by a court of law. In biblical times divorce was an independent action taken by a husband against his wife. It was a time-honored way of disposing of an unwanted wife.

The procedures outlined in Deuteronomy 24:1-4 were intended to regulate the practice of divorcing a wife. If she were guilty of some indecency (literally, "the nakedness of a thing," 24:1), or if the husband simply disliked her (24:3), he was required to give her a bill of divorce when he put her away. With this certificate in hand she was free to remarry another man without being accused of adultery. The husband was forbidden from ever remarrying her after she became the wife of another man who might also divorce her or who might die. For Moses, the abomination was not divorce but remarrying the first wife.

Most folks in Jesus' day were of the opinion that husbands had an inalienable right to put away their wives. They only differed over the permissible grounds for doing so.[4] Jesus came at the question of divorce from a quite different angle. Unlike the rabbis, he did not raise legal questions concerning the delivery of the certificate of divorce or the payment of the separate fee. He asked questions about the will of God. His answer was that God intended marriage to be a lifelong commitment. Marriage was not a temporary, romantic fling; it was a permanent union between husband and wife. Therefore, wives are not to be dismissed at the whim of the husband.

Jesus' teaching on divorce undercut all those who thought they could safely dispose of an unwanted wife and still be righteous because they fulfilled Moses' command to give her a certificate of divorce. In a later incident in the Gospel, Jesus accuses his opponents of misreading Moses' instructions about the certificate of divorce (Matt. 19:1-9). They mistook these directions as God's endorsement of divorce. Jesus insists that the rules in Deuteronomy 24:1-4 did not condone divorce. The opponents counter, "Why did Moses command to give the wife a certificate of divorce and to put her away?" (19:7). Jesus corrects them by pointing out that Moses did not command, he only permitted this because of human hardness of heart (19:8). The stipulations in Deuteronomy 24:1-4 were only a compromise. God's plan for marriage is therefore not to be found in Deuteronomy 24:1-4 but in the beginning, in Genesis 1–2.

Jesus faults his opponents for misunderstanding both the Scripture and God's will. He says that God joins marriage partners together; and if that is so, who are we to attempt to sever that union (Matt. 19:6)? God is the Lord of the marriage, and a husband may not act as if he were the lord and discard his wife to suit his fancy. God's will, as Jesus reveals it, invades all areas of life, including what is culturally accepted and legally permitted. You shall not divorce because divorce is adultery, a violation of the marriage. A piece of paper does not nullify the permanence of a marriage.

The exception clause. Only Matthew's Gospel includes an exception to the absolute prohibition of divorce. Matthew 5:32 reads, "Everyone who puts away his wife except on the grounds of *porneia (parektos logou porneias)* and marries another commits adultery" (see Matt. 19:9). This so-called exception clause has been the occasion of much debate. What does the word *porneia* mean in this passage, and what is the exception? A number of explanations have been offered.

Some claim that Jesus forbade divorce for anything less than adultery. Matthew added the exception clause as a parenthetical remark to make explicit what would have been assumed by Jesus—namely, that adultery broke the marriage bond. Others argue that Jesus maintained that divorce itself was adulterous (19:9), not just divorce followed by remarriage. Matthew added the exception clause to free some divorces from the charge of adultery. If a wife was guilty of fornication, the husband who divorces her is not guilty of adultery for divorcing her. If she has already violated the marriage, she cannot be made an adulteress if she is divorced.

An increasing number of scholars now argue that the Greek word *porneia* refers to sexual sin in general and does not mean "unchastity" or "fornication" in this instance. Instead, the word is said to refer to marriage within the forbidden degrees of kinship. The rules concerning such things are found in Leviticus 18:1-23; 20:10-21. The word can be used to refer to what Jesus would consider an unlawful union. The marriage of Herod Antipas and Herodias, the former wife of his brother who was still alive, was a notorious example of such an unlawful union. Divorce in such cases is justifiable because God does not recognize this marriage as valid in the first place. The exception clause refers to an exceptional case of marriage within forbidden degrees. If this view is correct, then Jesus does not allow for divorce except in the most abnormal circumstances.

Divorce and adultery. In Matthew 5:32, Jesus says that the husband who divorces his wife makes her an adulteress and that anyone who marries her is an adulterer. Adultery, by definition, is the violation of the marriage bond. If Jesus says that one is guilty of adultery when one remarries after divorcing or having been divorced, it means that he believes that the marriage relationship continues to exist. Regardless of what legal action a spouse might take to end a marriage, Jesus assumes that the one-flesh union continues.

This attitude toward remarriage would seem to compound the woes of the wife who has been put away. If she married again, she would be guilty of adultery. How was she to survive? But Jesus was not concerned here with the fate of the divorced woman. He was concerned with expressing the will of God concerning marriage and divorce. These statements underline in broad strokes the permanence and sanctity of marriage. No action a man might take and no court decision can ever truly sever the marriage relationship in the eyes of God. In *The Book of Sirach* 25:26, one finds the advice that if your wife does not go as you would have her go, you should cut her off from your flesh. Jesus claims that one can never disentangle the one-flesh unity created by marriage, and the spouse can never be considered a disposable appendage. The marriage relationship can be dissolved only by death.

This assertion would have met with an ever greater shocked response in Jesus' day than in ours. The essential words of a bill of divorce were: "Behold thou art permitted to any man."[5] The whole point of the procedure was to avoid the charge of adultery on anyone's part should they ever remarry. Jesus' audience must have been as amazed by this saying as we would be if he said to us, "anyone who sells his car and buys another is guilty of theft."

Divorce is clearly a breach of God's will for marriage. It is a sin that springs from our hardness of heart. Consequently, the church needs to take a stand against the rising tide of easy divorce in our society. Many enter marriage today without any sense of it being a lifelong commitment. The vows have been changed from "to have and to hold as long as we both shall live" to "as long as my spouse meets my needs and I feel fulfilled." Christians are not to be conformed to this world and this includes its indifference to the marriage vow. God hates divorce, because, like all sin, it destroys. Divorce in particular is like an atomic bomb that leaves deep emotional craters and strikes all kinds of innocent bystanders with the fallout. This is why God hates divorce and why the divorced person usually hates divorce; it is another contribution to chaos in the world. While God hates divorce, the church must always be mindful that God does not hate the divorced person. Therefore, the church must balance on a tightrope by proclaiming both the sanctity of marriage while proclaiming God's full mercy and forgiveness to sinners who violate that sanctity.

Swearing oaths (5:33-37)

The swearing of oaths was a prevalent practice in Jesus' time that was much abused. In the Old Testament, one was directed to swear by the name of God (Deut. 6:13; 10:20) as a sign of one's allegiance to the Lord rather than to idols. The law of Moses strictly forbade false oaths because they cheapened the name of God (Exod. 20:7; Deut. 5:11; 1 Kings 8:31-32). In keeping with his demand for a greater righteousness (Matt. 5:20), Jesus prohibits all oaths and vows. By forbidding oaths, Jesus ignores the practical problems that this demand creates for his disciples in a society that required oaths in all manner of disputes. With the advent of the reign of God, all such concerns have been superseded.

Jesus rejects the use of oaths for at least four reasons. First, he requires that his disciples speak the truth as a matter of course. Disciples are to be trustworthy because they are inwardly pure in heart, not because they have uttered an oath. Others may advocate total honesty; Jesus demands it and insists that the honest truth needs nothing to shore it up. The use of oaths either implies that one is normally untruthful or that one need only be truthful when swearing an oath.

The common misuse of oaths and vows by the masses is a second reason Jesus renounces them. At that time many people tried to avoid using the name of God in oaths and vows out of a pious fear. They wanted to duck the grim punishment attached to profaning God's name, so they concocted substitute oaths using indirect terms such as "heaven," "earth," "Jerusalem," "the altar," and "the temple" (see 23:16-22). Jesus scorns this attempt to skirt around the name of God with makeshift oaths. He demonstrates from the Scripture that all substitute terms directly involve God. To think that one who swears by the temple, altar, or heaven has not sworn by the living God is nonsense. He denounces swearing by one's head (or one's life) because it presumes that we, not God, have authority over our lives. It is all a legal mirage. God cannot be evaded through the use of word games. An oath is an oath no matter how roundabout the reference to God.

A third reason Jesus rejects oaths is his affirmation that humans are bound to God in all of life, not just when we call upon God as a witness. We will be held responsible for every word we utter (12:36), not simply those uttered in an oath. A lie is a lie whether we swore that it was the truth or not.

The last reason that Jesus rejects oaths is perhaps the most important. An oath is used to guarantee the truthfulness of a human statement and calls upon God as a supporting witness. Who are we to require God to notarize our fallible human statements? Oaths and vows essentially reduce God to an object of human manipulation. For Jesus, they are clear assaults on the majesty of God.

Retaliation (5:38-42)

The law of Moses stipulated an eye for an eye and a tooth for a tooth (Exod. 21:23-25; Lev. 24:19-20; Deut. 19:21).

This principle served to rein in reckless blood vengeance such as Lamech's boast, "If Cain is avenged seven times, then Lamech seventy-seven times" (Gen. 4:23-24). We have a lot of modern-day Lamechs who boast: "I don't get mad; I get even." The purpose of the law of the eye and the tooth was to provide a civilized alternative to otherwise unlimited blood-feuds. It was designed to limit retribution. It allows one to get even within limits, but it does not *require* one to get even.

Once again, Jesus takes us beyond the written law to recapture the will of God. When he says do not resist evil or the one who is evil, he does not mean that we are to buckle under to the evil. He means that we are not to resist violently. Do not retaliate with violent aggression. Paul echoes the same idea in Romans 12:19: "Beloved, never avenge yourselves but leave it to the wrath of God" (see 1 Thess. 5:15). The fact that the opponent is designated as "evil" reveals that God will handle things in due time; but that is the prerogative of God, not humans. Therefore, Jesus prohibits even measured retaliation and gives three illustrations of how one is to respond to being wronged (when one is struck, sued, and coerced) and one illustration of how one is to respond when a fellow victim asks for help.

Turning the cheek. Striking another on the cheek has always been a way to humiliate an enemy (see Job. 16:10; Lam. 3:3). But Jesus specifies that one had been struck on the *right* cheek. That detail indicates that one has been slapped with the back of the hand; that is the height of insult. The other person is not just bullying us but baiting us. Recognizing this fact changes the popular picture of what Jesus is teaching. He is not simply urging us to turn the other cheek when someone aims a blow at us. He instructs us to turn the other cheek when someone assaults us with insulting violence. Such a calculated indignity was considered to be at least four times as injurious in the rabbis' legal discussion on damages for violence. They ruled:

> If a man cuffed his fellow he must pay him a *seal* [four *zuz*]. R. Judah says in the name of R. Jose the Galilean: One hundred *zuz*. If he slapped him he must pay 200 *zuz*. If [he struck him] with the back of his hand he must pay him 400 *zuz*.[6]

Jesus' teaching does not simply call for passive resistance but summons us to overcome the natural reflex to repay violence with violence. Violence, even when it is intended to shame us, is to be met with good will and calm composure. Disciples are to endure injury rather than to inflict it.

What does turning the other cheek do? First, it snuffs out the spread of violence. To strike back only extends the life of the evil. But turning the other cheek also changes the power initiative. To strike someone with the back of the hand is to treat him or her as an inferior. When the victim turns the other cheek, the assailant is then forced to slap him with the open hand as he would an equal. The victim has, in effect, made the one who would demean him to respond to him as a fellow human. It says to the higher-ranked individual, "Try again. I am a human being like you. I will not be shamed by you."

Being sued. Jesus says if someone wants to take your tunic in a lawsuit, let him have your outer garment as well. His audience must have consisted of the poorest of the poor who had only the clothes on their backs to give as collateral for a loan. Jesus does not say to give the other the cloak but to "let him," that is, offer it to him. The law, however, specifically forbids a plaintiff from claiming the cloak of another.

> If you lend money to one of my people among you who is needy, do not be like a moneylender; charge him no interest. If you take your neighbor's cloak as a pledge, return it to him by sunset, because his cloak is the only covering he has for his body. What else will he sleep in? When he cries out to me, I will hear, for I am compassionate. *Exodus 22:25-27;* see *Deuteronomy 24:10-13, 17*

If we translate this saying into modern parlance, Jesus is saying: If someone sues you for your coat, let him have the shirt off your back as well. To respond in this way would mean that you literally become naked. Is Jesus telling us to give up our rights completely?

Paul espouses a similar idea in his outraged response to the news that the Corinthians were suing one another in pagan courts. He says that to have lawsuits at all is a disaster, "Why not suffer wrong? why not be defrauded?" (1 Cor. 6:7, RSV). Why not, since love is able to endure all things (1 Cor. 13:7)? But the situation of the Corinthian Christians was different from Jesus' audience. The Corinthians had the power to sue others. The situation Jesus envisions is that of a destitute peasant who is being hounded by a merciless creditor. The peasant is seemingly powerless. He is not well connected and cannot appeal to civil rulers for justice. He cannot start a revolution or appeal to a Zorro or a Robin Hood to redress the wrong, nor should he. But is Jesus telling those who are down and out just to grin and bear the injustice? Does he expect his disciples to be docile and uncomplaining when they are treated harshly, in the hopes that they might win the good will of the oppressor?

In our opinion, Jesus is not telling people simply to submit to injustice. His counsel to give the creditor all one's clothes completely changes the power initiative. To understand how this is so, one must imagine the setting in a small Palestinian village. A man waylays another and demands his cloak to insure payment of his debt. The debtor proceeds not only to give him the cloak but also to offer him all his clothing. If he accepts the offer, the result will be a poor person standing naked before him and the entire village who has gathered to take in the scene. In a shame/honor society, the creditor would be the one who is publicly shamed as a cruel and pitiless man. If the debtor were to start undressing in the middle of the street, is it not likely that the lender would desperately urge him to stop? Would he not plead with the debtor, "Please, keep your clothes on!" In this situation, who now has the power? Jesus' teaching gives some measure of dignity and power to those who have none.

Going the extra mile. To be compelled to go one mile is a technical expression for being impressed into government service. Animals could be commandeered for the official mail, and people and animals could be required to help soldiers carry their sixty- to eighty-pound packs. Being compelled to go one mile was a hated form of Roman exploitation for Jews who lived under their rule.[7] Note that a "mile" is a Roman measurement.

The background of this saying has unfortunately been neglected so that the radical nature of Jesus' demand has been domesticated into "going the extra mile." "Going the extra mile" may mean anything from giving 110% in an effort to being more kind than is expected. But Jesus applied this saying to the hated enemy who was seen as devouring the nation. It would be like telling a member of the PLO to carry the bag of an Israeli commando an extra mile, or vice versa.

T. W. Manson comments: "The first mile renders to Caesar the things that are Caesar's; the second mile renders to God the things that are God's."[8] Caesar requires that we surrender our services for one mile. God requires that we meet oppression with kindness. The rules are Caesar's. A believer's response to rules is the possession of God's realm, and Caesar has no power over that. When we are exploited, Jesus advises that we take the power initiative and ask, "Is there anything else I can do to help you?" Again, one changes the power and perhaps the enemy.

Giving and lending to those who ask. Jesus instructs his disciples to give to the one who asks and to lend to the one who wants to borrow. Giving was most often used as a means of exercising power over the recipient. The benefactor becomes a patron, and the recipient becomes a client who must then repay the kindness in some way. Jesus transforms this attitude. He claims that the true benefactor is someone who gives without expecting any return from the person who receives. The one who helps others with no strings attached will be repaid by God who is the source of all gifts.

If one's goal is to accumulate wealth, this teaching is a piece of bad advice. If one's goal is to live peaceably with others as members of God's household where all are to have their fair share, then it is urgent counsel. This is the way things are to work under the reign of God.

Loving your enemies (5:43-48)

The last antithesis contains one of Jesus' hardest sayings: "Love your enemies and pray for those who persecute you." One writer complained that it was humanly impossible to obey this word: "How can one expect a person to love an enemy who has harmed him or killed a member of his family?"[9] It is hard enough sometimes to love loved ones, let alone neighbors across the street. Does Jesus really expect us to love enemies and to pray for their welfare? Many people decide that he cannot really mean what he says about enemies, or they simply ignore it.

Nowhere does the Scripture instruct us to hate our enemy, but hatred for the enemy has always been taken for granted as normal and quite acceptable. Saul's contrite response to David demonstrates this sentiment, "If a man finds his enemy, will he let him go away safe?" (1 Sam. 24:19; see 2 Sam. 19:5-6). Most assumed that one was obligated by God to love the neighbor but certainly not the enemy. Again, Jesus calls us to a higher righteousness. The life of discipleship is not simply the lifestyle of the average person or the average church member. Jesus commands us to love both our neighbor and our enemy.

There is a difference between loving and liking. Jesus does not say that we need to like our enemy or to like what he does.

But love entails that we are concerned about the welfare of another. It means that we will do things that will benefit and not harm the other. We should also note that love and hate do not necessarily have to do with our emotions. Love when contrasted with hate in the Hebraic idiom can simply mean to favor or to prefer. To hate means to disfavor or to snub. We may say that we do not feel any hatred toward our enemy, but we may keep only to our friends and shun or discount those whom we do not count as friends. If we love our enemies, we will reach out to them and seek to include them in our circle.

Three reasons. There are three reasons Jesus commands that we love our enemy. First, he points out that it is God's way. God shines the sun and sends the rains indiscriminately on both the good and the evil (5:45). God showers love even on those who do not love him. God uses goodness to move sinners to repentance (see Rom. 2:19). A. M. Hunter writes: "To return evil for good is the devil's way: to return good for good is man's: to return good for evil is God's."[10] Anyone who claims to belong to God should be following God's ways, not the devil's or man's ways. To love your enemy and pray for those persecuting you is to become a child of the Father (on the meaning of this idiom, see the discussion on 5:9 above). Those whom Jesus addresses have themselves already experienced God's gracious love and gifts. Jesus has just pronounced them blessed and has promised the kingdom of God as their inheritance. If they are going to accept this blessing from God, then they are expected to do for others what God has done for them.

Second, Jesus insists on the love of enemies because it is the only way to overcome hatred. Hatred only begets hatred. Hatred writes off an enemy who may be transformed. When Jesus was traveling through Samaria, messengers were sent on ahead to a village to find a place to stay for the night. The Samaritans snubbed the disciples because they were on their way to Jerusalem. James and John entreated Jesus: "Lord, do you want us to call fire down from heaven to destroy them?" (Luke 9:54). The "sons of thunder" wanted Jesus to do what the prophet Elijah once did (2 Kings 1:12). They wanted him to destroy the town, so to speak, simply because it had refused them hospitality. Jesus rebuked them for their spirit and shortly thereafter told a famous parable about a Samaritan (Luke 10:25-37).

But what if Jesus had done as the disciples asked? What would have happened when the gospel went out to Samaria? The story recorded in Acts 8 would probably have been much different. When Philip spoke of Jesus to the crowds in Samaria, they probably would have said, "Wasn't he the one who terrorized one of our villages?" Jesus did not do what the disciples asked, and many Samaritans responded to the gospel with great joy.

There were probably some Christians who hated Saul when he was filled with malice and breathing threats and murder against the church. Who would have guessed that he would become apostle Paul, filled with the Spirit and preaching the gospel of love and forgiveness? The one who treats us as our enemy today may become our brother or sister tomorrow. Jesus says to treat them today as our brother and sister.

A third reason that Jesus gives for loving our enemies is the fact that the principle of an eye for an eye might be good enough for tax collectors and pagans, but it is not good enough for disciples. If you love only those who love you and greet only those who greet you, it is simply a business deal: "You scratch my back; I'll scratch your back." With this approach, every act is calculated and valued for what it might get us in return. If that is the way disciples live their lives, how are they any different from anyone else—even those they might classify as notoriously wicked? If disciples are the salt of the earth and the light of the world, then they must be different. They are to love one and all as God has loved them.

Be perfect. Jesus tops off this section of the Sermon on the Mount by telling us to be perfect. It seems that he gives us another impossible command. But is it so impossible?

The Greek idea of perfection was that something was without a flaw. Or it applied to self-acquired virtue. For the Hebrew, something was perfect if it fulfilled its purpose. The adjective in the Hebrew means to be complete, wholehearted, sincere, or true, and is usually translated *blameless*. One scholar writes that, in the biblical mentality, "the perfect person is in sincere right relationship with God and therefore open to the work of love which God wills to accomplish in him."[11] The term does not refer to religious perfection. It is used of Noah in Genesis 6:9. It is part of God's charge to Abraham to walk in his presence and be blameless (Gen. 17:1). It is part of God's charge to Israel in Deuteronomy 18:13: "You shall be blameless before the Lord your God." It is how God describes Job to Satan (Job. 1:8).

The essence of being perfect is to be in right relation to God. One cannot be a little perfect or half perfect; it is all or nothing. It is complete submission to God's absolute claim on us. God does not want our best effort at something that is unattainable, but he does want our total engagement and commitment.

Questions for Further Reflection

1. Why do you think Jesus stresses that he did not come to abolish the law?

2. How do Jesus' teachings on murder, adultery, divorce, and oaths challenge tradition?

3. How should we respond to our enemies?

4. What does Jesus mean by the word "perfect" (v. 48)? Is this command possible for us to obey? How does this command confront our spiritual complacency?

➠ Action Step

Identify the various life experiences in 5:21-48. How can you apply Jesus' teachings to your current life situation?

4

THE GENUINENESS OF KINGDOM CITIZENS

Matthew 6:1-18

The Sermon on the Mount began by portraying the essential elements of a disciple's character and the influence for good one could have who exhibited kingdom characteristics. This was followed by a description of the "righteousness" of the scribes and Pharisees. Kingdom righteousness is righteousness unlimited. Such authenticity must penetrate beyond our actions and words to the heart, mind, and motives, and must control us even in the secret, hidden places.

Three closely related examples are chosen from the cardinal components of Jewish piety: almsgiving, prayer, and fasting. The Sermon's overriding theme—the greater righteousness demanded of kingdom citizens—is continued by contrasting the true piety Jesus expects of his followers with the hypocritical piety of the scribes and Pharisees. Those characterized by genuineness are concerned primarily with relationship to God and his approval rather than the applause of men and women.

Almsgiving (6:1-4)

The foundational concern in Jesus' warning is against practicing piety before others for the purpose of drawing attention to these "acts of righteousness." This principle unites all three illustrations in this section. An initial reading of verse one might appear to contradict Jesus' earlier command: "Let your light shine before men" (5:16). Both verses speak of doing good works and in both the objective includes being seen by others. Yet, Jesus commands it in 5:16 and prohibits it here. Jesus is addressing two very different problems. In the first he is concerned with human cowardice. The second addresses our tendency toward vanity. A. B. Bruce rightly notes that "we are to show when tempted to hide and hide when tempted to show."[1]

Our good works must be public so that our light shines. Our private piety must remain secret so we will not boast about it. The motives for each are the same, namely the glory of God. We keep our piety secret in order that glory may be given to God. We do good works openly and let our light shine so that those who observe such actions may glorify our heavenly Father.

The point of Jesus' teaching is that those who do such things to gain a public reputation for piety get exactly that, but God will grant no additional reward. But when pious acts are practiced so that God alone knows about them, he will bestow an appropriate reward: the opportunity for further practice of genuine piety.

Jesus' first example relates to the giving of alms (6:2-4). To give money for the poor was one of the most sacred duties of Judaism. The apochryphal book of *Tobit* says, "It is better to give alms than to treasure up gold. For almsgiving delivers from death, and it will purge away every sin" (12:8-9).

Avoiding hypocrisy (6:1-2)

Jesus indicates that kingdom citizens are not to give to the needy as the hypocrites who sounded a trumpet to call attention to their benevolence and thus receive the praise of others. It is unclear if the trumpets referred to were literal or symbolic. It has been suggested they might refer to the noise and clang of throwing money into various collection receptacles. The point of Jesus' words, however, is quite clear. His followers should offer a private gift, knowing God will provide the proper reward.

Kingdom citizens must be different from the hypocrites. In the Greek world *hypocrite* was the ordinary word for an actor or one who wore a mask. The New Testament, however, offers the larger meaning of a spiritual pretender, one who plays the part of righteousness, without possessing the inner reality (see Matt. 6:2, 5, 16; 7:5; 15:7; 22:18; 23:13-15, 23, 25, 27, 29; 24:51). One second-century rabbi declared that nine-tenths of all hypocrisy in the world could be found in Jerusalem. But the problem remains present with us as well.

We rarely set out at the beginning of the day deliberately planning hypocrisy. But people rather easily accept a role assigned to them by society or government or business or religion. Without thinking, they perform various kinds of acts or duties in the name of tradition. When we accept the dualism between our own deepest sense of righteousness and that called for by the general public, then we have become maskers or hypocrites. Jesus calls for consistent genuineness.

The right and left hand (6:3-4)

Those who give to be seen and admired have been paid in full. No reward remains. The Greek term for "reward" had a technical commercial usage indicating a completed payment with a receipt. E. Schweizer observes that "only in acts of charity (in Judaism) was their hope of receiving both honor in this life and a heavenly reward later—the capital remaining invested in heaven while the interest is enjoyed on earth."[2]

Rather than calling attention to one's acts of charity, one should not even let the left hand know what the right hand is up to. It is not necessary to suggest how this literally might take place.[3]

God will see the kindness and provide the appropriate reward at the right time. This means we are not only not to tell others about our giving, but in some sense we are not even to tell ourselves. We must not be self-conscious about our giving, for self-consciousness can quickly deteriorate into self-righteousness. Instead of looking for a reward from others or from ourselves, we look to God alone.

What, then, is the reward that the heavenly Father bestows upon the secret giver? John Stott answers:

> It is neither public nor necessarily future. It is probably the only reward which genuine love wants when making a gift to the needy, namely to see the need relieved. When through his gifts the hungry are fed, the naked clothed, the sick healed, the oppressed freed and the lost saved, the love which prompted the gift is satisfied. Such love (which is God's own love expressed through man) brings with it its own secret joys, and desires no other reward.[4]

Praying (6:5-15)

This section, like the one before and the one to follow, in vivid and intentionally humorous imagery paints a picture of the hypocrite's way of being religious. It is the way of ostentation. To poke fun at the first-century Jewish Pharisees is easy. To reflect on our own Christian pharisaism is less than humorous, for we too, if we are honest, like to boost our own egos and blow our own trumpets whether in acts of giving, praying, or fasting.

Warning about public displays (6:5-6)

In this second example, Jesus portrays two men at prayer. He contrasts genuineness and hypocrisy based on their motivation for praying and its reward. There is a place for public prayer, but there is something particularly distasteful about praying ostensibly to God when one is actually "praying" in order to be heard by others and build one's own reputation. The public prayer of kingdom citizens should represent the overflow of a vibrant personal prayer life.

The devout Jew would recite the *shema* (from Deut. 6:11 and Num. 15) three times daily (see Acts 3:1). According to Jewish custom (like the Moslem practice today), if you were in the streets at this time it was proper to stop, turn toward the temple, and pray. Apparently some planned to be in a conspicious place when it was time to pray. On busy street corners they would lift their hands in displays of public devotion for passers-by. Like those who focused attention on their public acts of giving, these hypocrites have been paid in full.

The disciples, in contrast, are to enter a private place—a storeroom or broom closet—and close the door. There they may address their Father who is "unseen" (NIV) or "there in the secret place" (NEB). He will at that time give the appropriate reward.

Warning about meaningless words (6:7-8)

Jesus adds a second warning. One must not "babble" or use "meaningless words." The term employed for "babbling" refers to useless ongoing repetitions. The KJV's translation of "vain repetition" puts the emphasis at the wrong place: on the vanity rather than the repetition, though both are involved. Behind the word for "babble" is the practice of the heathen who developed long lists of divine names, hoping that by endless repetition they might somehow invoke the divine name of the "true god" and receive what they desired. It was thought that if people could pronounce correctly the name of a god then they could manipulate that god.[5] Unfortunately, this has its counterpart in the eloquent phraseology used by some Christians today. We need to remember that God prefers the simple "Father" (see v. 9).

Likewise, we must remember that we do not acquaint God with our needs when we pray. We remind ourselves of these needs and recognize our deeply dependent attitude of trust that can receive his mercy in times of need (see Heb. 4:14-16).

The model prayer (6:9-13)

After correcting false understandings of prayer, Jesus offers his disciples a model for genuine praying. This prayer is frequently called the "Lord's Prayer." However, this title more appropriately fits Jesus' high priestly prayer in John 17. This model prayer could be designated the "disciple's prayer."

Without question this prayer is the best known and most frequently quoted of any other prayer. Athletic teams say it, often for "good luck," before ballgames. Winning teams celebrate their victories by quoting this prayer. Little children repeat it at certain gatherings. The early church members, by the second century, were commanded to recite the prayer three times daily, thinking that such repetition enhanced spirituality (*Didache* 8:3—a manual of the Christian church on service order). In light of verses 7-8, these practices appear quite ironic. We must ask ourselves what is the appropriate use of the model prayer? Why did Jesus teach the disciples to pray in this manner (notice the key word "how" in v. 9)?

The same prayer, in a somewhat shorter form, is found in Luke 11:2-4 where Jesus responds to a request from his disciples: "Lord, teach us to pray just as John taught his disciples." Matthew's account includes three parts that relate to God and his kingdom and four requests for believers' everyday lives. There is a question whether the prayer, like other parts of the Sermon (see Chapter 1) relates to the present or future aspects of the kingdom.[6] It is better to take the first three petitions in light of the future consummation and the remaining four as related to God's actions in our lives at the present time.[7] Each aspect of the prayer has implications for both the present and the future. The prayer summarizes Jesus' teaching about the kingdom of God.

F. F. Bruce, quoting C. F. Hogg and J. B. Watson, says the prayer:

> can be repeated in less than half a minute, contains petitions which range from the common bread-and-butter needs of our breakfast tables to the age-long purposes of God; puts God's glory first, our needs second, does not rule out material matters as too trifling to pray about, yet insists on the supremacy of the spiritual, and emphasizes the basic condition of the disciples' enjoyment of the Father's forgiveness.[8]

The concern for God's glory (6:9-10). The first three petitions in the prayer express concern for God's glory in relation to his name, rule, and will. If our understanding of God were of some impersonal force, then of course he would have no personal name, rule, or will to be concerned about. But Jesus does not refer to an impersonal "unmoved mover" or "ground of being"; instead he addresses God as "our Father in heaven." His divine fatherhood points to the truth that he is a personal God.

Jesus' concern in the opening address is not with proper protocol but with truth. When we recognize God as our loving heavenly Father, we can approach him in genuine humility, confidence, and devotion.

The Greek word for "Father" (pater) translates the Aramaic Abba. This type of intimate address was virtually unknown in first-century Judaism. He is our heavenly Father (Matt. 10:32-33; 12:50; 15:13; 16:17; 18:10, 14, 19, 35; 20:23; 25:34; 26:29,

39, 42, 53). The disciples are encouraged to break with the formality of liturgical phrasing and draw near to God as a loving parent. No doubt such an approach to God must have initially sounded irreverent to Jesus' hearers. Such intimacy, however, invites our deepest concerns and our loftiest praise. It tells us God is accessible, personal, and caring as opposed to some unfeeling, impersonal force. The words "our" and "in heaven" indicate the prayer should reflect the corporate concerns of kingdom citizens. That he is a "heavenly" Father points to his majestic greatness and his transcendent sovereignty.

The three phrases "hallowed be your name," "your kingdom come," and "your will be done" are probably similar forms of what is basically the same petition: to each the words "on earth as it is in heaven" are applicable. To "hallow" the name of God means not only to reverence and honor God, but also to glorify him by obeying his words. The petition regarding the "kingdom" reflects the desire for the final establishment of God's sovereignty, the consummation of the divine rule over the lives of men and women, which had been inaugurated in Jesus' incarnation.

The meaning of the phrase "your will be done" points to his purpose in history as well as the ethical will of God that kingdom citizens must obey. This ethical aspect of God's will is common in Matthew's Gospel (7:21; 12:50; 21:31). T. W. Manson observes, "There is a sense in which the Kingdom comes whenever and wherever God's will is acknowledged and obeyed on earth."[9] Without undercutting the eschatological emphasis of the petitions, we can say God's name is hallowed and God's kingdom comes when God's will is done on earth.

God's care over our lives (6:11-13). The first part of the prayer places the emphasis where it belongs: on God and his kingdom program as believers worship him and obey his will. The order has particular implications for the priorities of our lives and contrasts the self-centeredness of secular and worldly value systems. Our priority is not our name or our will, but God's. This does not mean our cares are unimportant to God. The pronouns "your" (in the first half) and "our" (in the second half) do, however, indicate the proper priority and balance in our praying. Now Jesus focuses attention on God's care for our personal concerns. Since God is "our Father in heaven" and loves us, he is concerned for the total welfare of his children and desires for us to bring our needs trustingly to him—our need of food, forgiveness, and deliverance from evil.

The first request for "our daily bread" is for the supply of personal needs, for what we need to sustain bodily life (v. 11). The Greek adjective translated "daily" is not found elsewhere in the New Testament. The word is best interpreted in terms of measure rather than time. The request thus signifies the bread that we need to be given us today (day by day).[10] God's faithful provision of manna that could not be stored (except on Friday) for a future day (Exod. 16:4-5) provides the background for this understanding. Jesus wants us to know that God responds to our needs day by day.

The second petition is for forgiveness (v. 12). Our failures put us in God's debt since we owe him complete obedience. In Jesus, people saw and heard something greater than a brilliant teacher; they met God dispensing grace and forgiveness. Jesus' death for our sins destroyed the barriers between ourselves and God. His work on the cross provided "forgiveness of sins" (Matt. 26:28). This forgiveness is the foundation of the new covenant community inhabited by Jesus' disciples. However, the old world still affects the new community. Thus the need for forgiveness, the restoration of fellowship with God on a daily basis. Like bread, forgiveness must be received daily. Like bread, forgiveness must be shared. The request for forgiveness follows our willingness to forgive others. Those who will not forgive show their inability to receive forgiveness. We cannot be reconciled to God without reconciliation in our personal relationships. The reminder that only the forgiving can ask for forgiveness is reinforced in verses 14-15.

Requests three and four state the negative and positive side of the same concern. "Lead us not into temptation" probably means "please do not let us fail the test" or "do not let us give in to temptation." The phrase should not be understood as asking God not to tempt us or asking him not to allow us to be tempted (see James 1:13). It may point to the kind of faith and loyalty needed for life's crucial tests (Matt. 26:41). Regardless, it is a recognition of our need for divine enablement in this life as we encounter various temptations from the evil one. In spite of the fact that we are members of the new community as kingdom citizens, we must recognize our own vulnerability and deep dependence on God's strength. The parallel request asks for protection from Satan or evil in general. The aim of Satan, the "evil one," is to destroy the faith of the people of God.

The NIV and other modern language translations do not include the concluding doxology. It is commonly recognized that this was a later liturgical addition to give the prayer a proper ending (most likely based on David's prayer in 1 Chron. 29:11-13). A few decades after the publication of the Gospel of Matthew, the doxology appears in the *Didache's* version of the model prayer. Whether or not it was part of the original prayer, it certainly forms an appropriate conclusion.

The importance of forgiveness (6:14-15)

To conclude the teaching on prayer, Matthew includes Jesus' sayings on forgiveness. This demanding phrase expands verse 12, stating that God's forgiveness as it relates to us depends on our willingness to extend forgiveness to others. It is not a scorecard arrangement where God only forgives us as many times as we forgive others (as if we could merit forgiveness). Rather Jesus stresses that those who have received forgiveness will forgive others.

Fasting (6:16-18)

The third religious duty is now addressed: the practice of fasting. The Pharisees fasted twice a week on Mondays and Thursdays. John the Baptist and his disciples also fasted regularly (Matt. 9:14). Jesus himself fasted for forty days (Matt. 4:2-11). In Acts we see the early church fasting (Acts 13:2; 14:23). Yet in Matthew 9:14-17 Jesus defends its disuse by his disciples as long as he was with them. In light of this, what is the significance of Jesus teaching on fasting at this point in the Sermon?

The meaning of fasting

First, we must ask, what is fasting? It is an exercise in self-denial and self-discipline to abstain from food. Going without food or drink for any period of time is a form of fasting. Thus we call the first meal of each day "breakfast" since it "breaks a fast" of the previous night during which we ate nothing.

Prayer and fasting are often grouped together in Scripture. This does not mean all praying is accompanied by fasting, but it means when we need to seek God's help for special blessing or guidance we turn aside from food to seek God (see Ezra 8:21). Also, we should fast in order to be able to share with others in need, as well as to practice personal self-discipline.

The manner of fasting

Jesus' emphasis is not on the meaning of fasting, however, so much as it is on the manner of fasting. The entire section focuses on the genuineness of kingdom disciples in contrast to ostentatious hypocrisy. The first is motivated by humility and divine reward; the second by vanity and human recognition. Jesus' instructions exhort his followers not to call attention to their practice of fasting.

The Pharisees' practice was to disfigure their faces and look dismal. Probably they smeared their faces and beards with ashes in order to look pale, sad, and "holy." Their goal was to be noticed by all. Their reward was the admiration they outwardly received. Jesus' directions emphasize a contrasting practice. He says, "But when you fast, do not look somber . . . ."

Jesus was not suggesting something unusual. He assumed they would wash and groom themselves daily. The disciples should follow a regular routine so others would not suspect they were fasting. As with giving and praying, "the Father who sees what is done in secret will reward you." Those who fast must not advertise their spiritual practices by outward signs of deprivation. Ironically, the hypocrites made themselves unrecognizable in their attempt to be recognized.11

The Didache (16–18) demonstrates a major misunderstanding of Jesus' words. It says, "Let not your fasts be with the hypocrites, for they fast on Mondays and Thursdays, but you fast on Wednesdays and Fridays." Jesus' point that fasting should be a private and voluntary practice before God has been missed entirely. It shows how easy it was then (and is now) to misapply Jesus' teachings.

Today we are prone to fall into the same hypocritical trap. How desperately we sometimes long for recognition of our "pious acts." How easily we misread Jesus' words with the same mistaken wooden literalism and thus miss the essence of his teaching. Giving, praying, and fasting are all good practices. We can, however, turn these acts of serving others and seeking God into self-serving displays. Motivation is the key. Do we seek to please God or ourselves and others? We can fool others, and even ourselves at times. We cannot, however, fool God. God hates hypocrisy, but loves genuineness. Only when we focus our worship and service Godward will our giving, praying, and fasting—as well as our other pious deeds—be pleasing in his sight.

Questions for Further Reflection

1. What three aspects of worship does Jesus discuss in 6:1-18?

2. What do you learn about genuine and hypocritical motives from Jesus' teachings about these three aspects of worship?

3. Why are your motives just as important as your deeds?

4. What part of your Christian experience is sometimes play-acting?

5. What do you think about the practice of fasting? Should this be a regular aspect of your Christian life?

➠ ACTION STEP

Read again and meditate on the paragraph on prayer (6:5-15). List three practical teachings that will impact your own personal prayer life.

5

THE SECURITY OF KINGDOM CITIZENS

Matthew 6:19-34

In this segment of the Sermon, Jesus unfurls his views on wealth and what he expects disciples to do with their money. The subject of money is always a bit touchy, and Jesus offers some financial counsel that is unwelcome to many. First, he tells the disciples not to pile up wealth on earth because it is ultimately a bad investment (6:19-21). Then he says that those who are full of light are generous with their possessions (6:22-23). Next, he warns disciples not to fool themselves into thinking that they can devote themselves to both God and money (6:24-25). Finally, by showing that God knows and provides for our needs (6:25-34), he points out the futility of worrying about worldly security.

The First Choice: Heavenly or Worldly Treasures (6:19-21)

From Jesus' perspective, there are two places one can choose to store up treasure: heaven or earth. Jesus opts for heaven for the simple reason that treasure stored there will last longer. The realm of heaven is not subject to the ravages of moths, worms, or thieves. Treasure in heaven is incorruptible (1 Pet. 1:4). The vaults are more secure, the banker more reliable. To invest one's life in this world by accumulating and hoarding possessions is like speculating in the junk bonds of an already bankrupt company. It is to invest in something that is constantly threatened by such things as decay, depreciation, and theft. Everyone knows that you can't take it with you, but Jesus says it isn't worth taking with you even if you could.

Jesus does not go into specific details about what he means by storing treasures in heaven or on earth. We do find clues elsewhere in his teaching. Jesus' parable about the Rich Fool (Luke 12:13-21) provides a graphic example of the peril of storing treasure on earth. We must be honest, however. If we were to read about this man in a magazine—something other than a parable of Jesus entitled the Rich Fool—we probably would not consider him as all that foolish. He has the pleasant problem of a bumper crop and bulging barns. His solution is to build bigger barns to store his harvest and all his good things. According to our conventional wisdom, this decision does not seem to be ill-advised. Here is a man who has foresight and who carefully maps out his future security. To us, he looks like a savvy businessman. He does not appear to be a crook. He is not a miser. He is one of those fortunate souls who is able to see the big picture and make daring business deals that pay off in big financial dividends down the road. If we are honest with ourselves, this prosperous farmer is someone we are more likely to envy than to dismiss as a fool. It is God's verdict that he is a fool, not ours.

God's vantage point

Jesus helps us see life from God's vantage point. And from God's angle of vision, the man is a complete fool. He spent his last day alive selfishly planning for a long future. He was careful and astute when it came to preparing for his comfort and security in this life but careless and stupid in preparing for the life to come. He thought that good things and plenty of them would bring him happiness and that it was time to stop and smell the profits. He was going to settle back, take it easy, and enjoy the fruits of God's bounty, which he now claimed as his own. Notice that he asks himself what he is to do with "my crops," "my grain," and "my good things" as if they were all his. He forgot that everything we humans possess on God's earth comes to us on temporary loan from God. He thought he was so shrewd in planning for tomorrow. But he did not look far enough into the future. He forgot that the mortality rate remains steady at one hundred percent. He forgot about God who is apt to interrupt us right in the middle of money making. He forgot about others as well. It never dawned on him that he could solve his silo problems by storing some of God's plenty in the mouths of the needy.

Storing treasures

Jesus concludes the parable with the image of storing treasures, "So it is with one who stores up treasures for himself and is not rich toward God" (Luke 12:21). The image of storing something up in heaven is found in Deuteronomy 32:34: "Have I not kept this in reserve and sealed it in my vaults?" This passage refers to a store of evil works that God retains and will one day avenge. James gives fair warning that the rich will howl for the miseries coming upon them (5:1-4). Their wealth will be corrupted, their fine designer clothes moth-eaten, and their gold and silver corroded. That corrosion will be a testimony against them for their bad investment. They laid up treasure for the last days, and it shall eat their flesh like fire.

Jesus says that there are much better investment opportunities. Instead of gathering earthly assets, we can store up something with God that will reap a heavenly reward, not punishment. In Luke 12:33, he implies that one can make deposits in God's celestial bank by giving alms: "Sell your possessions and give to the poor. Provide purses for yourselves that will not wear out, a treasure in heaven that will not be exhausted." In Matthew 19:21, he tells the rich man seeking the key to external life: "Sell your possessions and give to the poor, and you will have treasures in heaven." According to Jesus, the way to pile up wealth in heaven is to give it away on earth.

Jesus is not asking us to impoverish ourselves. He does not renounce the good things of this world. He is very concerned that people have the basic material necessities for life. But he knows that things can exercise a tyranny over the ones who possess them or who want to possess them. We are sadly mistaken if we think that a greater abundance of material things will lead to a greater abundance of life. It doesn't. Nor does it lead to a greater sense of peace and security. The more a person has, the more he or she has to worry about moths, worms, and robbers. When worry takes over, we become confused about what is really important in life. The danger is that possessions will end up possessing us. That is why Paul advises in 1 Corinthians 7:29-31 that one should "possess all worldly goods as though one did not possess them" (authors' translation).

Jesus' wisdom about how to store up lasting treasure clashes head-on with the wisdom of our world. The investment counselor of our day recommends raking in as much earthly treasure as you can. The jokes are that money may not buy happiness, but at least it finances the illusion. Or, those who believe that money can't buy happiness simply don't know where to shop. This kind of philosophy is what drives our generation of the Grand Acquisitors. Jesus' philosophy that it is more blessed to give than to receive or to amass a fortune meets with scorn in many quarters.

One look at the empty lives of those with great possessions helps us see that Jesus is the one who has the truth. All that wealth can do is acquire the pleasures of eating and drinking and other sensual delights (Luke 12:19). It cannot afford cheerfulness of spirit nor freedom from sorrow. Witness the many rich who are full of sadness and despair and wretchedness. Why is it that several famous athletes who had earned millions recently confessed that they turned to cocaine and alcohol to try to overcome depression? Material wealth cannot fulfill our deepest spiritual needs. Nor can it purchase eternal life.

To store treasure in heaven, on the other hand, is to make an eternal investment. The fool in the parable learns too late that the only things worth having and storing up are those that death cannot snatch from us. He left a legacy for his heirs to squabble over after the funeral. But he did not leave a legacy of benevolence. Jesus casts a spotlight on our everyday values from the vista of eternity. From there, our covetousness looks pretty silly. Those who invest only in themselves, in their own security, comfort, and pleasure, have made a bad bargain. They will wind up spiritually and morally bankrupt. Jesus causes us to think about how we would want people to eulogize us. Do we want people to say at our funeral, "He was the richest man I knew"? Or would we want them to say something about our kindness and generosity?

Jesus concludes this first saying about money: "Where your treasure is, there shall your heart be." What a person treasures reveals everything about that person's heart, because the heart is the center for making decisions. Jonathan Swift wisely commented that it is one thing to have money on your mind; it is another to have money in your heart. From Jesus' perspective, earthly treasure is a snare because it causes us to give our hearts to this transient, material world. We can become consumed with the consumption of things, things that are here today and gone tomorrow. They can easily slip through our fingers, so we become absorbed by concerns for their security. The result is that we cannot be pure-hearted, focused entirely upon God. And when our heart is not directed toward God, we are at risk of losing everything.

The Second Choice: Light or Darkness (6:22-23)

A single eye

The second saying about the use of money is a metaphor about the eye as the lamp of the body. A lamp emits light. As a lamp, the eye is depicted as radiating the light that resides within a person. The light source is the heart—where a person's treasure is (6:21).

Many translations of 6:22-23 imply that Jesus is concerned about the health, soundness, or clarity of the eye (see the RSV; NRSV; NASB). But these translations are somewhat misleading. The KJV is more accurate with its literal rendering, "If your eye is single . . . ; if your eye is evil." But what does it mean to have a "single" eye or an "evil" eye?

In our culture, we have various expressions about the eyes. Sometimes they describe a person's physical condition. For example, someone who is red-eyed or bleary-eyed is tired. Sometimes we refer to the eyes to describe a person's feelings or character. Someone who is moon-eyed or dreamy-eyed is in love. Someone who is sharp-eyed is crafty. Someone who is cross-eyed or cock-eyed has a distorted view of reality. Someone who is bug-eyed is very excited. In the Old Testament, we find references to people being single-eyed. That single-eyed person is someone who is generous or liberal (see Prov. 22:9).

Paul uses the noun form of the word "single" to refer to those who contribute to liberality (Rom. 12:8), to praise the Macedonians for their wealth of liberality (2 Cor. 8:2), and to urge the Corinthians to be generous as well (2 Cor. 9:11, 13). James uses the adverb to refer to God who gives generously (James 1:5). When Jesus refers to someone having a single eye, he means that person is someone who gives to others with open-hearted generosity. The warm heart shines through the warm eyes.

The opposite of the single eye is the evil eye. The evil eye has nothing to do with witchcraft. It refers to a stingy or a begrudging spirit (Prov. 23:6; 28:22; see Deut. 15:9). The same expression occurs in Jesus' parable of the generous vineyard owner who paid all his laborers the same wages regardless of the hours they worked. When the workers who put in a full day's labor bitterly complained, the owner asked them: "Is your eye evil because I am good?" The RSV renders it, "Do you begrudge my generosity?" (Matt. 20:15). This crew wanted to have more for themselves, or for the others to have less.

The presence of light

According to Jesus, a single eye is evidence of the presence of inner light. To be generous, one must be full of light. If one is not charitable, it raises the question of whether there is any inner light. Jesus' point is that the lack of charity with one's possessions is a sure sign that darkness reigns within. It is one thing to be in the dark but worse to have the darkness in you. Being generous, however, is a sign that kingdom citizens have moved into the world of light that floods the whole being.

This saying about the eye describes the disciples who do what Jesus commanded in 5:42. He said that they are to give to those who beg and to lend to those who ask. He also says that they are to give alms without letting the left hand know what the right hand is doing (6:3). When they do that, it is clear evidence of the light that shines within them. According to Jesus, you can see it in their eyes.

The Third Choice: God or Mammon (6:24)

First love

Jesus continues the theme about money with his declaration that it is impossible to serve both God and mammon. The imagery comes from the world of slavery. It was possible for a slave to be the property of two different owners, even to be rented out to another, but one can imagine how this situation would put the slave into a bind. One owner might command this; the other, something else. The upshot will be that the slave will inevitably be more faithful to one master than to the other. Jesus says, "he will love the one and hate the other." It is not that the slave will actually hate the other master. "To hate" is a Hebraic idiom that means "to love less" or "to be indifferent" (see Luke 14:26; Gen. 29:31-33; Deut. 21:15; John 12:25). What Jesus means is that one master will get more devoted service than the other. In this case, it is going to be either God or mammon who gets slighted.

Scholars disagree on the exact derivation of the word mammon. It is possible that it comes from a Hebrew word that means "to trust" and that it was used to refer to whatever one places one's trust in for security. We do know that in Jesus' world the word *mammon* was used for property in general. It had a neutral meaning and was not considered to be something that was tainted with evil. It simply referred to wealth or anything of value. It is striking that when Jesus uses the term it always has a negative sense. For him, mammon is hazardous material.

Once again, Jesus differs from the majority opinion of his day (and ours). For most, the pursuit of wealth was not something that conflicted with piety. Profit and gain were not considered evil, nor was the quest of these things considered inconsistent with obedience to God's will. It was assumed that one could be equally devoted to making money and to God. But Jesus argues that one cannot give one's heart to both. God and mammon are pictured as two totally different taskmasters. They give conflicting commands. If we obey mammon, we will disobey God. If a person is dedicated to the making of money, God will inevitably be pushed to second place or even lower. A heart given over to mammon means that one will not have the heart to serve God. Jesus insists that loyalty to God must come first and that it must be undivided. Just as we cannot follow a road that forks, we cannot serve God and mammon at the same time. God requires a single eye and single service.

Both/and or either/or?

The problem is that people try vainly to pull off a delicate balancing act. We try to satisfy both God and our own selfish desires. But Jesus knows that those who are totally preoccupied with the pursuit of earthly fortune will become wholly indifferent to the demands of God. The reason is that mammon makes us deaf to God's commands. It blinds our spiritual judgment and hardens the arteries of compassion. Jesus started off this section notifying us that our ultimate destiny is tied to where we invest our hearts. If we give our hearts to mammon, we are due for more than just heartache. Its darkness will engulf our souls, and it will purchase nothing more for us than a place in the outer darkness. The only escape from enslavement to the rule of things is to submit entirely to God's rule over our lives.

The Fourth Choice: Security or Anxiety (6:25-34)

Dealing with worry

We humans spend half our days worrying about something. In the last teaching of this section, Jesus tells us to quit being so troubled. But what exactly does he mean? Is he advocating a happy-go-lucky lifestyle: "Don't worry, be happy"? Is he saying that we need not plan for the future? Does he bid us to become indifferent to life?

The fact is that some worry is good. It helps us meet deadlines. It stirs us to prepare for the next assignment. It nudges us to get medical checkups. The worry that Jesus warns against is the destructive kind. It is the anxiety that so easily turns into distress or torment. And anxiety about money matters gets most of us in its grip. Jesus is directing us not to become so frantic about our concern for material prosperity that we are too distracted to function. The root idea of the verb "to be anxious" in Greek means to be pulled apart. We are not to allow our lives to become so wrapped up with material well-being that we go to pieces when it is threatened or taken from us. Jesus is not discouraging forethought but rather nervous anxiety. Sowing, reaping, and gathering, or toiling and spinning can be done with anxiety, or they can be carried out with faith.

God's care

Jesus seeks to calm the fears of those who worry about an uncertain future. First, he tells us to ponder the world of flowers and birds. He paints on his canvas a rich landscape that illustrates God's care for his creatures. But, like all good paintings, we only get the message if it engages our imagination. Jesus says that God feeds the birds without them having to sow or reap. The more cynical among us might respond that birds spend most of the day hunting for food, and they do not always get enough to eat. But the picture of a heavenly Father feeding the birds is intended to trigger in our imaginations an ideal world that contrasts with the hurry-scurry of our own. In our world we develop complex networks and schedules to sustain ourselves. In the bird world they neither sow, reap, nor amass food in barns, but they get fed. Then Jesus asks us, if the heavenly Father takes care of the birds, are we not of more value to him than they? Will the Father not also take care of us?

Jesus awakens our imaginations with a picture of God's fatherly care for the birds. The second stage of the argument pictures the lilies of the field that neither toil nor spin and yet they increase. Jesus adds that these wildflowers are not merely clothed. They are clad with a grandeur that cannot be matched even by Solomon, decked out in all his glory. Jesus then switches the direction of this argument by calling these breathtaking flowers "the grass of the field."

It is now clear that Jesus is not being sentimental about birds and flowers. The "grass of the field" was a standard image for something worthless. Jesus deliberately stresses the paradox between the glorious beauty of the flowers and their final insignificance. Today, the beauty of the flowers stun those walking through the fields; tomorrow, they are thrown into the oven as fuel. If the heavenly Father is so lavish in clothing field flowers that are destined to be consumed in an oven, how much more gracious will he be with humans?

When we look at the canvas Jesus has painted for us, we see a God who makes clothes for the flowers and prepares meals for the birds. We must then ask ourselves if our anxious concern to provide for ourselves is really necessary. And Jesus would have us conclude at least five things.

Five conclusions

First, it is unnecessary for us to be so anxious about our lives. Jesus tells us not to worry because we need not worry. The heavenly Father bestows his care on the birds and the flowers. If God takes care of them, how much more will God take care of us who are made in his image, even if we are of little faith? God knows that we need food and clothing (6:32). Jesus' argument accords with the psalmist's wonder, "What is man that thou art mindful of him, and the son of man that thou dost care for him?" (Ps. 8:4, RSV). He assures us that God is mindful of us and cares for us.

Second, Jesus makes it clear that it is futile to be anxious. He good-naturedly quips, "Who can add one cubit to his span of life (or to his height)?" No one grows by worrying about his height. No one prolongs his life by worrying about prolonging life. The truth is that worry and workaholism actually shorten life and make it miserable while it lasts. One can ruin the present by living in anxious concern about the future. Someone has said that worry is a stream of fear trickling through the mind. If it is not halted, it will cut a channel into which all other thoughts will drain.

Third, Jesus argues that it is basically pagan to be so anxious. To seek after "all these things" as if they were the most important things in the world is labeled a heathen pursuit (6:32). The Gentiles crave all these things because they do not know God (see 6:7) and are deceived about what is crucial in life. They also suppose that they can insure their security for the future by their own strength and efforts. The disciples' awareness of God's love should cast out all anxiety and help them set their priorities straight.

Fourth, to be anxious about the future is an affront to God. It discloses our basic mistrust of him. Our worry says that we really do not believe that God is a heavenly Father who is sufficient to provide for us today and tomorrow and to deliver us through death. If we pray to God to give us our daily bread, why should we frantically seek after it or try to hoard as much as we can for ourselves? Jesus urges the disciples to live in trust and to leave the unknown in God's hands. A later rabbi echoed the same sentiments when he said: "Whoever has bread in his basket and asks, 'What shall I eat tomorrow?' is none other than the one of little faith." When we are anxious for tomorrow, we are also being presumptuous. We assume that God will grant us another day. Jesus says, do not be anxious about tomorrow; for when tomorrow comes, it will have its own worries.

A simple poem may help us understand what Jesus is saying because it uses similar imagery:

Said the robin to the sparrow
I would really like to know
Why those anxious human beings
Rush about and worry so.

Said the sparrow to the robin,
Well, think that it must be
That they have no heavenly Father
Such as cares for you and me.
—Anonymous

Fifth, being anxious for what we shall eat and wear is rooted in a fatal illusion that our real needs are physical. Why devote your attention to clothes that soon wear out and go out of style? Worry about such things is like a warning light that should alert us to a spiritual problem. It means that our faith in God and our fidelity to his commands are clashing with our selfish concern for material security. Dr. Martyn Lloyd–Jones comments that Jesus is telling us not to worry about anything, but since we probably will anyway, then worry about something significant. Worry about our relationship to the Father and whether he truly rules over our lives.[1]

We have contended that the immediate context of all these sayings has to do with generosity. How is anxiety over material security related to this issue? It is simple. Those who constantly worry whether they will have enough for themselves will not be very generous to others. If we trust in God to provide for our needs, we will be more ready to help in providing for others.

The Ultimate Choice: The Kingdom and Its Righteousness (6:33)

Jesus concludes this section by exhorting us to seek first the kingdom of heaven and its righteousness, and all these things will be added. That does not mean that if we seek first the kingdom of heaven then we are due all kinds of material bounty. We cannot say to God, "I sought your kingdom first; now give me all the riches you promised." If we are truly seeking God's kingdom and its righteousness, then we will be indifferent to material prosperity (see Phil. 4:12). Jesus is not promising selfish people a sure-fire plan for getting all they want from God. He is assuring those who submit themselves to God's rule that they will have all they need.[2] The emphasis of this saying is on the "first." Jesus does not deny that we have physical needs, but he is making it a question of priorities. We can think of all kinds of things that might come first in our lives before the kingdom of God. We might say to ourselves, "First, I must do this; then I must do that." The kingdom citizen's first task, however, is to seek wholeheartedly the kingdom of heaven. If we are doing that, we cannot be consumed by the anxious accumulation of material things. Then we will also know true security and peace of mind.

Questions for Further Reflection

1. What is the primary teaching of 6:19-34?

2. Why are earthly treasures more inviting than heavenly ones?

3. How can we escape worrying about such things as food and clothing?

4. How can we reconcile the teachings in this section with our duty of providing for our dependents?

ACTION STEP

Reflect on the meaning of seeking first God's kingdom and righteousness in 6:33. Identify three practical ways the application of this teaching can affect your life.

6

THE RELATIONSHIPS OF KINGDOM CITIZENS

Matthew 7:1-12

Relationships with others are an indication of one's own self-understanding. Realizing the limitations, particularities, and complexities of our own lives should help us to be more understanding of others. Jesus' words regarding judging others do not suggest we should endorse all beliefs and lifestyles. Rather, Jesus calls for discernment. This section addresses kingdom citizens' relationships to one another (7:1-6) and their relationship to God (7:7-11). It concludes with a summary statement that climaxes Jesus' ethical teaching (7:12).

Relationships to One Another (7:1-6)

Judging (7:1-2)

Jesus tells the disciples "Do not judge, or you too will be judged." "Judge" in this context carries the connotation *condemn*. We are exhorted in other contexts (e.g. 7:6, 15-20;

18:15-17) to make value judgments and to offer rebuke when necessary. Jesus' words here, however, are concerned with faultfinding and condemning attitudes. These are often issued without all the facts in a situation or without a realistic awareness of one's own failings. The very least one can expect in such cases is to "be judged" with equal or greater severity by others.

Often these verses supply the basis for those who want to be affirming and accepting of all people and things. We must remember that Scripture regularly instructs believers to evaluate carefully and make choices between good and evil. Disciples are to test everything (1 Thess. 5:21) and must watch out for those who are immoral (1 Cor. 5:9), who masquerade as angels of light (2 Cor. 11:14), and who teach false doctrine (Phil. 3:2; 1 John 4:1).

Jesus is concerned about condemning attitudes. The grammatical construction of verse one, as often in Matthew, probably points to God himself as the agent. Just as he will forgive those who forgive (6:14-15), he will condemn those who condemn. Those who take up the judging task usurp the place of God and thus become answerable to him. D. A. Carson paraphrases this verse: "Do not assume the place of God by deciding you have the right to stand in judgment over all—do not do it, I say, in order to avoid being called to account by the God whose place you usurp."[1]

Verse two supplies the theological foundation for the exhortation in verse one. To be faultfinding or censorious is presumptively arrogant; in fact it is to play God. Yet we must realize that not only should we not judge, but we are among the judged. We shall be judged with a more severe strictness ourselves if we dare to condemn others. When we put ourselves in the position of judge we cannot plead ignorance to the standards we are claiming to administer.

The proverbial saying is not a requirement to be blind, but an exhortation to be generous. We are not to suspend our critical powers but to renounce our presumptuous ambition to be God (by establishing ourselves as judges).[2] The verse condemns the ease with which we become judgmental of people who are different from ourselves.

Hypocrisy (7:3-5)

Verses 3-5 graphically illustrate the type of hypocrisy condemned in the first two verses. The illustration also reveals something of Jesus' humor (see also Matt. 19:24). With the use of a cartoon-type hyperbole, Jesus tells his famous parable about foreign objects in people's eyes, specks of dust or splinters on the one hand and planks or logs on the other.

The "speck" refers to a tiny splinter of wood or straw, something very minute. The "plank" refers to a large log or, more literally, a beam or rafter used in the building of the temple. The speck and the plank in the eye are found also in two rabbinic sayings, perhaps drawn from Jesus' words. Jesus does not indicate it is wrong to help a fellow disciple remove the splinter from his or her eye. It is, however, wrong for the one with a plank in his own eye to offer assistance. Jesus' concern is our meddling with "picky" problems while failing to handle our own more serious faults.

The parable illustrates another reason we should not judge. Because we are fallen sinners, even though regenerate kingdom citizens, we are in no position to stand over others.

The grotesque picture is ludicrous. Seeing someone carefully struggling with the surgical procedure of removing a speck from someone else's eye while his own vision is completely obscured by a huge plank is comical until it is properly understood. We are the ones with the plank. Our faultfinding with others is thus ridiculous. How quickly we are to exaggerate the errors in others and to minimize our own mistakes. Sadly, what we sometimes do is find our own glaring faults in others and so judge *them,* resulting in a hypocritical self-righteousness.

How hypocritical, in view of our own failures, to be concerned with the minor fault in someone else's life. Some have seen here the enormous offense of our own failure before God in comparison with the minor problems between people based on the account of the debtors in Matthew 18:21-35. Regardless, the point is clear. Jesus rebukes our self-promoting and censorious hypocrisy. This is the only time in the Sermon that the disciples are identified as hypocrites. The term is generally reserved for the leaders of the religious establishment in Matthew's Gospel.

The story taken in an unqualified sense would put an end to helping others with moral failures and personal struggles. Within the kingdom, censorious faultfinders are unhelpful. But when we, in a meek and humble manner, remove the plank from our own eyes, then we can responsibly help our brothers and sisters as needed (see Matt. 18:15-20; 1 Cor. 1:31; Gal. 6:1). The story is intended to restrict hypocritical correction of others rather than to restrict all helpful correction. Jesus calls for his followers to avoid prejudice, prejudgment, and stereotyping.

In sum, from Jesus' words in this section we recognize our limitations. First, we only know in part and never fully understand all aspects of a particular situation, such as the real motivations of others. Second, we cannot be completely impartial. Our emotional involvements with others often obscure our judgment and cause us to critique others merely at the emotional level. Third, we recognize that only God is competent and capable to administer judgment (see James 4:12). When we judge ourselves, and with God's enabling grace bring about changes and corrections in our lives, then, and only then, are we able to help remove the speck from our brother's eye. Helping our brothers and sisters at their point of need must be done with grace, mercy, generosity, and understanding.

Discretion (7:6)

Jesus has one more statement in this section. Verse six contains complex word pictures that are difficult to understand. He says, "Do not give dogs what is sacred; do not throw your pearls to pigs." This little parable is full of bizarre and shocking imagery that has perplexed commentators to no end.

In the first place, the picture is not quite clear (though the structure of the saying appears to be chiastic). It is the pigs that will trample the pearls beneath their feet. The dogs will turn and bite the hands that feed them. Yet the meaning is enigmatic. Throwing pearls to pigs is intelligible, even if not wise. Pearls appear a bit like peas or acorns and would deceive the pigs until they discovered the substitution. Giving dogs what is "holy" is more problematic. Some have said that the original Aramaic spoke of giving gold rings to dogs, since the words for "holy" and "ring" are quite similar in Aramaic. This would appear to make a fitting parallel to pigs and pearls.

Another suggestion is that "holy" is a reference to food offered in sacrifices. It is no help to treat the passage allegorically as the great thinker, Augustine, attempted to do, imagining that the text will suddenly become clear if we can only discover the deeper meaning of the terms *dogs, holy, pearls,* and *pigs*. Regardless, the picture warns against giving something valuable to completely inappropriate dogs and pigs and reaping the consequences.

Dogs and pigs traditionally were considered unclean and unpleasant and held in low esteem (see Exod. 22:31; 2 Pet. 2:22). The Jews employed both terms to describe heathen Gentiles (Matt. 15:26; Mark 7:27) and acted condescendingly toward them. With this background, it is most likely that Jesus is speaking of offering the "holy food" or "pearls" of the kingdom (the reference is primarily to the teaching of the kingdom) to unreceptive and hostile hearers.[3]

Similarly, Paul emphasizes that only the "spiritual" can understand spiritual teaching (1 Cor. 2:13-16). God's gifts are not to be laid open to abuse, or his truth to mockery. Jesus' point is that teaching should be given in accordance with the spiritual capacity of the hearers.

No doubt the saying could have been applied by some more restrictive group in the Jerusalem church as an argument against presenting the gospel message to Gentiles, certainly against fully accepting them into the church. Early in the second century it was used as an argument against admitting pseudo-believers and followers of the various religions of the Roman Empire to the Lord's Supper. The *Didache* includes this statement, "Let no one eat or drink of your Eucharist except those baptized into the name of the Lord, for, as regards this, the Lord has said, 'Give not that which is holy unto dogs'" (*Didache* 9:5). It would be anachronistic to read these later interpretations back into the ministry of Jesus. It is far wiser for us to read the parable in the context given it by Matthew (the only Gospel writer to report this saying).[4]

Thus it is unthinkable to take sacred food and give it to dogs or valuable pearls and offer them to pigs. Finding pearls unpalatable, pigs will trample them underfoot, and dogs will attack those who feed them. We must use wise discretion in sharing the truth of God with others. Jesus himself knew that it was useless to impart his message to some people: he had no answer for Herod Antipas when Herod questioned him (Luke 23:9). The passage gives us a balance for the teaching against judging. We need to use insightful discretion in preaching, teaching, and sharing the gospel. Discrimination is to be applied according to the attitude and receptivity of our hearers. Overexposure of sacred things to unprepared and unreceptive persons can create an adverse reaction. Finally, we must remember how God has patiently dealt with us, and we must likewise persevere with others.

Relationship to God (7:7-11)

That Jesus should move from our relationship with others to our relationship with our heavenly Father seems most appropriate. As Stott notes, "the more so because our Christian duty of discrimination (not judging others, not casting pearls before pigs, and being helpful without being hypocritical) is much too difficult for us without divine grace."[5] In many ways life in the kingdom is a life of prayer, trusting, and childlike communion with God. Now Jesus concludes this section with direct encouragement to pray.

Persistence in prayer (7:7-8)

Earlier in the sermon (6:5-15) we were introduced to a portion of Jesus' teaching on prayer. Now the teaching is expanded by means of the "how much more" argument that Jesus loved to use. He insisted on the believers' persistence in prayer and the assurance of answered prayer.

The present imperatives "keep on asking," "keep on seeking," and "keep on knocking" let us know that prayer is not a passive ritual in which we sometimes share our concerns and requests with God. By consistent and persistent prayer from the righteous hearts of the disciples the good things of the kingdom will be granted. The future tenses in the latter part of each phrase ("it will be given you," "you will find," "the door will be opened") provide assurance that what is requested from the heavenly Father will be answered.[6]

"Ask," "seek," and "knock" are metaphors for prayer, not separate exhortations. They are also found in rabbinic sayings as metaphors for prayer. These imperatives emphatically express a confident attitude toward the Father. Though sincerity is assured, no limitations or conditions are required, except the implied persistence. The prophet had similarly expressed: "You will seek me and find me when you seek me with all your heart" (Lev. 29:13). The requests are not requests to enter the kingdom. That relationship is presupposed. The request involves asking for and seeking the blessings of the kingdom.

In Luke 11:9-13 this teaching appropriately follows the parable of the persistent friend at midnight and the model prayer. The stress in each context (Matthew and Luke) is on God's willingness to answer prayer. The disciples learn that God's good gifts are available to those who characteristically and consistently "ask," "seek," and "knock." Jesus assures his followers that God is opening the way for what is otherwise impossible. Too frequently we modern-day disciples find the way closed because our requests are colored with selfish motives (James 4:2-3). Those who truly persist in prayer as Jesus described will not be spiritually impoverished, but will be blessed with the good things of the kingdom. Delays do not indicate divine reluctance. God may be using such a period to teach us patience and intensity in our prayers.

Confidence in prayer (7:9-11)

Prayer requires faithfulness. Those who keep on asking will receive and those who keep on seeking will find. Now, Jesus underscores the assurance believers can have in prayer comparing less-than-perfect earthly parents with the one perfect heavenly Father. The two illustrations are lifted from well-known Jewish arguments on the nature of prayer. These similarities inform us concerning Jesus' own synagogue education and his ability to identify wherever he could with right emphases and practices in Judaism.

Even the cruelest parent would hardly deliberately deceive a child asking for bread or fish by giving him a similar-looking substitute, whether an inedible stone or a dangerous snake. Jesus assumes the sinfulness of human parents, yet recognizes their willingness to give good gifts to children. Even sinful parents will not mock their children by giving a stone (round and smooth like a Palestinian loaf) instead of bread, or a snake (resembling an eel) instead of fish. Unlike the stone, the snake could be cooked and eaten, but it was considered an unclean animal (Lev. 11:29-31). A caring Jewish father would not deceive and defile his children by causing them to eat ceremonially unclean food. If earthly parents with their sinful nature will give good gifts to their children on request, *how much more* will a perfect heavenly Father give the good gifts of the kingdom to those who keep on asking. Such good gifts include righteousness, perfection, the will of God, and relationships in the believing community based on a common life of forgiveness and grace. These good things are not achievements but gifts graciously bestowed on those who ask, seek, and knock. The illustrations again strongly affirm for us God's fatherly kindness.

The Golden Rule: Ideal Reciprocal Relationships (7:12)

"So in everything, do to others what you would have them do to you, for this sums up the Law and the Prophets." The "so" serves as a bridge to connect this remarkable verse with the whole teaching of the Sermon so far. Jesus explains that what God desires to see in our lives is initiated by what he has already done for us and is even now doing for us. This forms the theological basis for the "Golden Rule." As William Barclay claims, "With this commandment, the Sermon on the Mount reaches its summit and its peak. This saying of Jesus has been called the "'capstone of the whole discourse.'"[7] Myron Augsburger agrees, noting, "This statement is no doubt the best known of Jesus' teachings and is the highest level of his ethical teaching."[8]

In its negative form, a similar saying can be found in many ancient cultures. Confucius said, "What you do not want done to yourself, do not do to others." The Athenian orator Isocrates (fourth century B.C.) taught, "Whatever angers you when you suffer it at the hands of others, do not do it to others." The Rabbi Hillel offered a similar response to a request that he teach the entire law while standing on one foot: "What is hateful to you, do not do to your fellow creature. That is the whole law; all else is explanation." Apparently only in the teaching of Jesus is the rule given in the positive form.[9]

The Golden Rule presents in a nutshell the "greater righteousness," the identifying characteristic of kingdom citizens. Jesus elevated the saying to a place of supreme importance as a summary of the revealed will of God.

Jesus' positive form moves us to active discipleship on behalf of others. It calls for us to do for others what we would welcome and appreciate being done for us. This shift from previous negative forms is significant. In its negative form the saying could be satisfied by doing nothing. The shift represents a move from passive justice to active kindness. In the positive form it calls for a far-reaching demand for other-centered living and unselfish love in action.[10] The law of love is the supreme expression of the ethical teaching of both the Law and the prophets. It is the ultimate guide for relationships in the kingdom.

Questions for Further Reflection

1. What is the difference between proper discernment and improper judging?

2. How does "judging" negatively impact relationships in the church?

3. Why can we be confident in our praying?

4. Why should we persist in our praying?

➠ Action Step

Identify the general subject of 7:1-12. List three practical applications from the truths taught here.

7

THE COMMITMENT OF KINGDOM CITIZENS

Matthew 7:13-27

Life is filled with calls for decisions. What will we do? Where will we go? What kind of work will we do? Daily we deal with decision after decision. This closing section is intended to evoke a decision from us—a response to Jesus. We will observe Jesus' calls for a rigorous discipleship (7:13-14); warning against false prophets (7:15-23); and commands that we choose the kind of foundation on which we will build our lives (7:24-27).

The Narrow and Wide Gates (7:13-14)

A note of urgency exists in these verses, and those that follow, which is often overlooked by those who make facile remarks about the Sermon as an ethical ideal.

The choice

Jesus issues a clarion call for rigorous discipleship; it is a matter of life and death. We are presented with two gates, which represent two ways—the two destinies from which we must choose. Jesus portrays his way as the path of life. The refusal to follow the straight road is disaster. A sharp distinction is drawn between mere religious activity and the authentic discipleship demanded of kingdom citizens.

Robert Mounce has reminded us that the idea of two ways is found throughout secular ethical literature.[1] Hesiod (the ancient Greek poet) warns that the way of wickedness is "smooth and near to hand," whereas the path to virtue is "long and steep and rough to begin with" (*Work and Days*).[2] Likewise, in the Old Testament Jeremiah records God's message, "See, I am setting before you the way of life and the way of death" (Jer. 21:8; see Deut. 30:19; *Didache* 1:1).

As we have noted before, the kingdom in Matthew is not entirely futuristic; it has been inaugurated at the coming of Jesus. Those who find and follow Jesus enter the life of the kingdom. Jesus commands his followers to enter through the narrow gate. The gate leads to the kingdom (a synonym for life in verse 14).

Matthew's usage combining both roads and gates is ambiguous. Does the road lead to the gate or does one enter through a gate onto a road? While the relationship between the road and gate is not clear, the essential idea is generally clear: one way is broad, the other is narrow.

Jesus distinguishes between two different gates and roads. The narrow gate/constricted road leads to life. The wide gate/spacious road leads to destruction (an allusion to final judgment). The way of righteousness set forth in Jesus' teaching represents the gate leading to life in the kingdom. This is the way that Jesus invites his hearers to enter now, so they can enter the kingdom at the journey's end (cf. 5:20; 7:21).

The outcome

These verses tell us that many enter into the broad way of destruction, but few will find the narrow gate. Some translations read "hard" instead of "narrow" in verse 14. The term *tethlimmene* means "pressed together," suggesting it is not the road for everyone. The statement that "only a few will find" this narrow road should not be interpreted as an answer to the question, "How many will be saved?" It is rather an invitation for kingdom citizens to act on what they have heard. Richard Gardner insightfully comments that "they have in fact *found* the way that eludes so many, and it is critical that they decide to follow it" (emphasis his).[3]

A Tree and Its Fruit (7:15-23)

False prophets

Jesus warned the people to "watch out for false prophets." This certainly suggests that he believed there were (and would be) such. They existed in the Old Testament; they were present during Jesus' times, and they have continued to bring havoc to the church throughout the ages (see Matt. 24:11-14; cf. 2 Pet. 2:1). John Stott comments:

> The history of the Christian church has been a long and dreary story of controversy with false teachers. Their value, in the overruling providence of God, is that they have presented the church with a challenge to think out and define the truth, but they have caused much damage. I fear there are still many in today's church.[4]

Another factor is clear: there is a standard of truth by which the false can be judged. Otherwise, the very notion of a *false* prophet would be meaningless (cf. Jer. 23:16-28). Jesus maintained that truth and falsehood are mutually exclusive. Kingdom citizens must avoid the attractive path of syncretism if they are to follow Jesus faithfully. Those who teach and preach falsehoods in God's name are false prophets, of whom the church must always beware.

Jesus described the false prophets as "ferocious wolves" in "sheep's clothing" (7:15). This description tells us they are not only devious and deceptive, but also dangerous, because they are in reality wolves. They appear to be like other members of God's flock. Like wolves, however, they really intend to devastate and devour the followers of Christ in order to satisfy their own needs (cf. Ezek. 22:27; Acts 20:28-29; *Didache* 16:3).

Certainly it is no accident that Jesus' warning about false prophets follows his teaching about the two gates. False prophets distort the true teaching of the kingdom and blur the gospel message, making it most difficult to enter the narrow gate. These pseudo-teachers are responsible for leading some people down the broad road of destruction that they claim does not exist; for they wrongly claim that all roads lead to God.

As deceptive as these false prophets are, the church can identify them "by their fruit" (7:16, 20). The fruit and tree imagery stresses the corresponding relationship between character and conduct, between doctrine and ethics. If there are no grapes, you do not have a grapevine. If the fruit is bad, you do not have a healthy tree. "Like root, like fruit" is the ancient saying. Right teaching must produce ethical uprightness. In reality, what we do reveals who we are.

It is important, if not imperative, to recognize that the standard by which wolves can be discerned includes both their false doctrine and the pattern of their lives. Because they are disguised, they are unsuspectingly welcome. Often their true character is not discovered until it is too late, and the damage has been done. The ultimate teaching of verses 15-20 is that, before God, people are what they do, not what they pretend to be. It is a tragedy that such men and women reappear through the ages and always find victims.[5]

The judgment

Verses 21-23 draw a sharp contrast between the mere talker and doer of God's will. Jesus claimed, "Not everyone who says to me, 'Lord, Lord,' will enter the kingdom of heaven, but only he who does the will of my Father who is in heaven." Having warned his audience about false prophets, Jesus addresses the issue of their destiny (see Luke 6:46ff.; 13:26-27).

Since a person's fruit reveals who he or she really is, it follows that simply calling Jesus "Lord" is not enough. "On that day" points to a scene at the final judgment (cf. Joel 2:1; Amos 5:18; Mal. 3:17-18). False prophets will protest on that Day of Judgment that they proclaimed the kingdom message and did kingdom deeds, listing their credentials as driving out demons and working miracles (cf. Acts 19:13-16).

Much to their surprise, they will be declared wicked people unknown to the Lord. Not only did these imposters claim to have confessed his name, they claimed to have invoked his power in ministry. In this case, however, such words and deeds helped constitute the "sheep's clothing" that enabled the ravenous wolves to identify with the sheep.

Their question (7:22) expects an affirmative answer. But Jesus will tear away the outer sheepskin and lay bare the ferocious wolf. In so doing, he will declare, "I never knew you" or, "I was never acquainted with you."[6] This scene underscores for us that neither confession of Jesus as Lord nor deeds accompanying such a confession in themselves constitute entrance into the kingdom. Only those who do what God desires will enter the kingdom of heaven. Judgment is based on living out the will of God, not on claims of kingdom activity.

Jesus never denies that false prophets could have performed "miracles" or "signs" (cf. Rev. 13:13-14). What he does deny is that he has or has had anything to do with them.

Thus, since he had not sent (commissioned) them in the first place, he now sends them away as having never known them.

Kingdom citizens are thus warned to be on guard against the insidious threat of false prophets. A sure defense is total allegiance to the person and ministry of Jesus the Messiah. This means entering the "narrow gate" (7:13), doing the will of the Father (7:21), and hearing and doing the words of Jesus (7:24-26). The false prophet of today still distorts the gospel of the kingdom. It may come in the form of legalism, universalism, or New Age syncretism. We must cautiously guard against this deceptive danger lurking in every Christian community.

Our calling involves being discerning and alert. Yet we should note in this context (7:15-23) that the ultimate verdict regarding the false teachers comes from the Judge, not the disciples. Our task is to make the message of the kingdom clear and relevant as we proclaim the gospel. The good news itself offers the best counter to the misleading and destructive message of the false prophets.[7]

The Wise and Foolish Builders (7:24-27)

Jesus concludes the Sermon on the Mount by telling a parable, a common practice among Jewish teachers. It is a story about two builders and the final condition of the houses they construct. In this concluding story we also find the answer to the questions previously raised or implied in this section (7:13-23). Who are the few who will walk the hard way and pass through the narrow gate (7:13-14)? Who are the ones who produce good fruit (7:15-20)?

Who will be welcomed on the last day (7:21-23)? Jesus' answer: "everyone who hears *these words of mine* and puts them into practice" (7:24, italics reflect emphasis of Greek text).

That one is like the wise person who built his house on the rock. In Luke's version (Luke 6:47-49), more attention is given to the process of building. Matthew, however, moves quickly to the details of the storm. Jesus pictures the two houses in two different locations: one on the rocky terrain of a mountainside, and the other in the valley on sand. The prudence of the wise man is shown in his putting into practice the teachings of Jesus. The house built by the unwise man is destroyed because he does not put Jesus' teachings into practice. A combination of wind, torrential rain, and swollen streams rushing into the valley brings destruction for this man.

The first house, on the other hand, withstands the storm.[8] Only when the storm broke and battered both houses with great intensity was the fundamental and fatal difference revealed. The house on the rock stood, while the house on the sand collapsed.

Similarly, professing Christians (both the true and the false) often appear the same. The contrast in Jesus' story is not between professing disciples and those in the world; rather, he is contrasting visible members of the Christian community. Both hear the Christian message. The difference is at a deeper level, at the place of foundations. The foundations may not appear to be different until the storms of life come along. Then those who *do* what they hear are revealed as genuine kingdom citizens.

John Calvin observed, "Sometimes a storm or crisis or calamity betrays what manner of person we are, for true piety is not fully distinguished from its counterfeit till it comes to trial."[9] If not, then surely the storm of the Day of Judgment will do so.

Neither good works, intellectual knowledge, or mere verbal profession can be substituted for the obedience of authentic discipleship. This is not to confuse "doing" for the grace of

God. Jesus, followed by the teaching of the apostles, stresses that only those who hear the gospel and confess Jesus as Lord will obey him, expressing their faith in their works. To claim to be a kingdom citizen, a follower of Christ, means that we understand the responsibility of translating what we know and what we say into what we do.

Those who seek first the kingdom must build their lives on a sure foundation. The choices between entering the narrow or broad gate, between following true or false prophet, between building our lives on rock or sand cannot be neglected. One way leads to life and entrance into the kingdom; the other to disaster and destruction. Life is filled with choices and decisions, but none more paramount than those offered here. What choice will you make?

Questions for Futher Reflection

1. What is the theme of each paragraph?
   - 7:13-14
   - 7:15-23
   - 7:24-27

2. What is common to all three?

3. What contrasts do you observe in these verses?

4. What distinguishes genuine prophets from false ones?

5. What do verses 21-23 teach about the final Day of Judgment?

➠ Action Step

Meditate on this final section. List four reasons for obeying Jesus' teaching. How can you begin to put this teaching into practice?

8

JESUS' WORDS FOR TODAY

Matthew 7:28-29

Matthew concludes the Sermon on the Mount by informing his readers of the initial hearers' response. The Gospel repeats these words in 11:1; 13:53; 19:1; and 26:1, in each case with a reference to the teaching just concluded. Each time Matthew adopts Old Testament language to indicate a formal transition in his Gospel (see Num. 16:31; Josh. 4:11; 1 Sam. 13:10; and Jer. 26:8).

The hearers of the Sermon included two groups: a primary audience defined as his disciples (5:1-2) and a secondary group called "the crowds" (7:28-29). Matthew claims the crowds were amazed and astonished. Their astonishment was not only over the content of his teaching but primarily his authority (see 13:54; 22:33). The teachers of the law quoted other rabbis to support their own teaching. These teachers, the scholars of the day, were professionally trained in the development, teaching, and application of the law. In contrast to their authority, which was grounded in human tradition, Jesus interpreted and applied the law with divine authority. For this reason, Jesus could declare the criterion for judgment to be his own words (7:24-27). He is much more than another scribe or teacher of the law; he is the Christ, the Son of the living God (see 16:16). In this final chapter, we will focus on who Jesus is and what his teachings mean for us today.

Who Is this Teacher?

During the past two thousand years, many people have attempted to drive a wedge between the Jesus of the Sermon on the Mount and the Jesus of the rest of the New Testament. This, however, is not possible. The bottom-line question the hearers and contemporary readers must ask is not, "What do you think of this teaching?" but, "Who is this teacher?" From the rest of Matthew's Gospel and the remainder of the New Testament we can answer this question.

The New Testament is our primary source of information about Jesus. He is the central figure of the New Testament and the focus of the Christian faith.

God's purposes were to be accomplished through a descendant of David. The people of God in the Old Testament looked forward expectantly to the coming of the promised king, their Messiah. The purposes of God had been revealed through a series of God's covenant promises (see Gen. 12:2; 2 Sam. 7:9; Jer. 31). In these covenants, God's intent for establishing his kingdom and for redeeming humankind was progressively revealed. These covenant promises found their ultimate fulfillment in Jesus Christ.

The Old Testament includes two different lines of teaching about the Messiah: He would be both King and Redeemer. Aspects of each purpose can be observed in the covenant promises and the prophetic portraits, though the details of the completion of these teachings remain somewhat unclear. The New Testament, however, interprets the Old Testament and announces that the promised Messiah had come in Jesus of Nazareth.

In identifying Jesus as the Messiah, the New Testament authors affirm an essential unity between the Old Testament and the New Testament.

The New Testament, which is rooted in the Old Testament, interprets and ampliflies the Old Testament, which Jesus acknowledged to be the Word of God and on which he based his teaching and ministry (see Matt. 5:17; John 10:34-35).

The Gospels indicate Jesus understood his mission in a way that ran counter to the assumptions and expectations of his contemporaries: both his followers and his opponents. One thing is for sure: Jesus understood his mission as a fulfillment of the Scriptures as indicated in his teachings and those of his followers, particularly Matthew.

The Teacher in Matthew's Gospel

The title (1:1) introduces us to the account "of Jesus Christ, son of David, son of Abraham." The genealogy that follows falls into three divisions of fourteen generations each. The structure is clearly symbolic, for some names are obviously omitted. Matthew distinguishes certain high points in his genealogy, particularly connected with Abraham, David, and the Exile. The name of Abraham recalls God's dealings and promises with the patriarchs; the name David points to all that the title "Son of David" signifies; and the Exile is a reminder of God's judgment on his people. In addition to the important recognizable names, there are names largely unknown. While Matthew emphasizes Jesus' kingship, he does not neglect that Jesus is "gentle and humble in heart" (11:29). It is thus significant that the "little people" are prominent in the genealogy. Some of these were women, some Gentiles, and others blatantly sinful (1:3, 5-6). Jesus' ancestry reveals that Matthew's Gospel, though primarily a Jewish gospel, exhibits an awareness that the redemptive work of Jesus is for all the world (28:18-20).

A worker of miracles

The Gospel's opening emphasizes Jesus' miraculous conception, the circumstances surrounding his birth, and focuses on Jesus throughout to the resurrection and final commission. Not only is Jesus presented as the fulfillment of prophecy in the life of Jesus, but he is seen as one who did mighty miracles. Of the twenty miracles recorded, about three-fourths of them are healings (4:23-25; 8:16; 14:35-36; 15:30; 19:2 indicate he characteristically healed many). Matthew brings both of these features together (see 8:17; 12:15-21) to show that his miracles fulfilled prophecy. More than spectacular acts, the miracles indicated that the one about whom the prophets prophesied had indeed come (11:2-6; 20–24). The spiritually perceptive would see that, in the miracles of Jesus, God was at work in a special way. The miracles were not primarily an external guarantee of the coming of the kingdom; it was one of the means by which the kingdom was inaugurated.

Son of Man

Jesus' greatness and identity as Son of Man can be observed in his claim that he will come in glory at the end of this age. The Son of Man, before his glorification, must suffer. Jesus' mission is often related to the title, "Son of Man." He has nowhere to lay his head (8:20), he has authority to forgive sins (9:6), and he sows good seed (13:37). "The Son of Man came not to be served but to serve, and to give his life as a ransom for many" (20:28; see 26:2, 24, 45). Also, Matthew's presentation includes the future coming of the Son of Man who will sit on the throne of glory (19:28; see 24:30; 25:31). The cross is at the essence of the mission, but there is also the certainty of his return.

Jesus preferred the title "Son of Man" to use for himself. Rather than a mere affirmation of Jesus' true humanity, "Son of Man" is a divine title of suffering and exaltation.

Son of David

The title "Son of David" was used as a messianic title and expressed a desire for a Messiah who would bring in the kingdom of David. Often, it was linked with militaristic expectations. The tracing of the origin of Jesus from David is a prominent feature of Matthew's genealogy. Even though the precise title appears only in *Psalms of Solomon* 17:21, the Jewish expectation of a Davidic King was too strong to make the use of the title questionable. Matthew brings out the importance of the title more clearly than the other Gospel writers. Matthew's purpose, which was to show how Jesus fulfilled the expectations of the promised Messiah, explains the reasons for his emphasis of this title.

Though the title is not featured in Mark or Luke, and is rarely mentioned in the rest of the New Testament (though cf. Acts 13:34; Rom. 1:3; 2 Tim. 2:8), Matthew uses the expression nine times. After the initial reference in the first chapter, Matthew always employs the expression as a title used by others, mostly in appeals to Jesus for help (9:27; 12:23; 15:22; 20:30-31; 21:9, 15). Matthew understands the title as an expression of hope. The Son of David, who was greater than David (22:41-45), would bring deliverance for those hopelessly in bondage.

Son of God

Matthew wants those with eyes and ears of faith to recognize Jesus of Nazareth as the Son of God.

This title is a key Christological title for Matthew employed at Jesus' birth (2:15), his temptations (4:3, 6), recognition by the disciples (14:33; 16:16), and his suffering and death (26:63; 27:40, 43).

Matthew used the theme of Jesus' sonship often. With the use of the title Jesus claimed special intimacy with the Father. He thanked the Father for hiding these truths from the wise ones of this world and revealing them to babes (11:25). In this special claim, "All things have been committed to me by my Father. No one knows the Son except the Father, and no one knows the Father except the Son and those to whom the Son chooses to reveal him" (11:27), Jesus acknowledged that he has the same intimate knowledge of the Father as the Father has of him. Jesus' relationship as Son of God is unique and as such is most significant for those who put their faith in Jesus.

Christ

Five times in the opening of his Gospel, Matthew used the title "Christ" (1:1, 16-18; 2:40). From the beginning, it is clear Matthew's focus was on the Christ. The questions, "Who is the Christ" or "What do you think of the Christ" are concerns of John the Baptist (11:20), the Pharisees (22:42; cf. 23:10; 24:5, 23), and the questioners/accusers at his trial (26:63-64, 68; 27:17, 22). At the zenith of the Gospel, we find Peter's great confession at Caesarea Philippi. It is revealed that Jesus is "the Christ, the Son of the living God" (16:16-20).

The Christ is not a name but a description meaning "the anointed one." Anointing is intimately associated with a divine commission to a royal, priestly, or prophetic ministry.

To acknowledge Jesus as "the Christ" was to affirm that the One from Nazareth was the Messiah foreseen by Old Testament prophets—the person commissioned by God to redeem his people.

Lord

The title "Lord" was associated with the ambiguities of the culture and context of Jesus' life. Sometimes, Jesus is addressed as "Lord" in the courteous rather than the spiritual sense (the NIV frequently translates the term as "sir"). But Matthew wants his readers to see the title is equivalent to the Old Testament name for God (*Yahweh*). "Lord" signifies that Jesus performed miracles with divine power (8:2, 6, 25; 9:28).

With this expression, the early church proclaimed the deity of Jesus of Nazareth. As Lord, he is "Immanuel," God with us (1:23). R.T. France is correct to note that Matthew portrays Jesus as "the man who fits no formula," but whose authority (28:18), declarations of forgiveness (9:2), demands for allegiance (10:37-39), and reception of worship (14:33) all depict him as "one in the place of God."[1]

The Significance of Jesus' Teaching for Today

Jesus came to prepare Israel, a people intimately familiar with their history and heritage, for the kingdom. His listeners shared a fundamental knowledge about God and his Word. Jesus initially taught those who had knowledge, not those who were ignorant. His teaching was not primarily intended to communicate the unknown, but to bring understanding and fresh insight. Likewise, for us today Jesus' teachings provide fresh insights concerning God and the kingdom and call for a complete allegiance from his followers.

We have seen that Jesus offered fresh understanding about God as Father (5:45-48; 6:9-13, 32-33). Because our heavenly Father will care for our basic needs, we are free to "seek first his kingdom and his righteousness."

Jesus also brought an expanded interpretation of the ethical teachings of his day. Christ's contemporaries thought his ethical principles novel not because of new content, but because of his approach to the issues.

Jesus called for an ethic of love (22:37-40). Yet, his ethic of love does not abandon rules. It does, however, shift the focus of attention from acts to intentions. We have observed how Jesus shifts attention from murder to the anger and hatred that lead to it (5:27-30). Jesus' teachings are concerned with inner motivation and not just deeds. He proclaimed, "Unless your righteousness surpasses that of the Pharisees and the teachers of the Law, you will certainly not enter the kingdom of heaven" (5:20). It is clear that Jesus wants kingdom citizens to be changed from the inside out.[2]

Jesus also enabled us to understand who he is. He is one with authority; he is God with us (1:23). This last chapter has summarized Matthew's portrait of Christ by surveying the key titles he employed. We must answer the same question Jesus asked of the disciples in Matthew 16, "Who do you say that I am?" This is the central issue.

He is the Christ, the Son of God. He has come as the Son of David to inaugurate the kingdom of God. When Jesus announced the kingdom of God is near, he was concerned with the reign and rule of God.

Jesus called on his listeners then and he calls on us today to enter, or receive, God's kingdom. He taught that God's sovereign authority over all things is to be affirmed. God's kingdom is a present reality for his people, as well as a future promise. Those who live under the Lordship of Christ, who do God's will, and who seek his kingdom wholeheartedly will experience the peace of God ruling and working in all the circumstances and events of life. May God grant to each of us the grace to be faithful seekers of the kingdom (6:33).

Questions for Further Reflection

1. What do we learn about Jesus from the following titles:
   - Son of Man
   - Son of God
   - Christ
   - Lord

2. Who do you say that Jesus is?

3. What is the significance of Jesus' ethical teaching for us today?

ACTION STEP

Identify the basic meaning of Jesus' "authority" for his followers. List three practical applications for us today from this essential teaching.

Appendix

Outline to the Sermon on the Mount

I. What Is the Sermon on the Mount?
Matthew 5:1-2

A. The Context of the Sermon
B. The Setting and Structure of the Sermon
C. Approaches to the Sermon
1. Utopian Ideal
2. Millennial Ethic
3. A Common Sense Guide
4. Binding on All or a Committed Few?
5. Teaching for the End Times
6. Internal Attitudes
7. Showing Our Need for Mercy
D. Kingdom Living Here and Now

II. The Character and Influence of Kingdom Citizens
Matthew 5:3-16

A. The Character of Kingdom Citizens (5:3-12)
1. Kingdom Blessings: The Beatitudes
a. Beatitudes in the World of Jesus
b. The Paradoxical Nature of Jesus' Beatitudes
2. Blessed Are the Poor in Spirit (5:3)
a. Who Are the Poor in Spirit?
b. Theirs Is the Kingdom of Heaven
3. Blessed Are Those Who Mourn (5:4)
a. Who Are the Happy Mourners?
b. They Shall Be Comforted

4. Blessed are the Meek (5:5)
    a. Who Are the Meek?
    b. They Shall Inherit the Earth
5. Blessed Are Those Who Hunger and Thirst After Righteousness (5:6)
    a. Who Are the Hungry and Thirsty?
    b. They Shall Be Satisfied
6. Blessed Are the Merciful (5:7)
    a. Who Are the Merciful?
    b. They Shall Receive Mercy
7. Blessed Are the Pure in Heart (5:8)
    a. Who Are the Pure in Heart?
    b. They Shall See God
8. Blessed Are the Peacemakers (5:9)
    a. Who Are the Peacemakers?
    b. They Shall Be Called Sons of God
9. Blessed Are Those Who Are Persecuted for Righteousness' Sake (5:10-12)
    a. Who Are the Persecuted?
    b. Reasons for Rejoicing

B. The Influence of Kingdom Citizens (5:13-16)
1. The Salt of the Earth (5:13)
2. The Light of the World (5:14-16)
3. The Doing of Good Works (5:15-16)

III. The Righteousness of Kingdom Citizens
Matthew 5:17-48

A. The Fulfillment of the Law (5:17-19)
1. Jesus Lived in Perfect Obedience to the Law and the Prophets (5:17)
2. Jesus Recaptured the Purpose of the Law and the Prophets (5:18)
3. Jesus Fulfilled the Promise of the Law and the Prophets (5:19)

B. The Higher Righteousness (5:20)
C. Examples of the Higher Righteousness (5:21-48)
1. Anger (5:21-26)
a. Namecalling
b. Sacrifice at the Altar
2. Adultery (5:27-30)
3. Divorce (5:31-32)
a. The Exception Clause
b. Divorce and Adultery
4. Swearing Oaths (5:33-37)
5. Retaliation (5:38-42)
a. Turning the Cheek
b. Being Sued
c. Going the Extra Mile
d. Giving and Lending to Those Who Ask
6. Loving Your Enemies (5:43-48)
a. Three Reasons
b. Be Perfect

IV. The Genuineness of Kingdom Citizens
Matthew 6:1-18
A. Almsgiving (6:1-4)
1. Avoiding Hypocrisy (6:1-2)
2. The Right and Left Hand (6:3-4)
B. Praying (6:5-15)
1. Warning about Public Displays (6:5-6)
2. Warning about Meaningless Words (6:7-8)
3. The Model Prayer (6:9-13)
a. The Concern for God's Glory (6:9-10)
b. God's Care over Our Lives (6:11-13)
4. The Importance of Forgiveness (6:14-15)
C. Fasting (6:16-18)
1. The Meaning of Fasting
2. The Manner of Fasting

V. The Security of Kingdom Citizens
Matthew 6:19-34

A. The First Choice: Heavenly or Worldly Treasures (6:19-21)
   1. God's Vantage Point
   2. Storing Treasures
B. The Second Choice: Light or Darkness (6:22-23)
   1. A Single Eye
   2. The Presence of Light
C. The Third Choice: God or Mammon (6:24)
   1. First Love
   2. Both/And or Either/Or?
D. The Fourth Choice: Security or Anxiety (6:25-34)
   1. Dealing with Worry
   2. God's Care
   3. Five Conclusions
E. The Ultimate Choice: The Kingdom and Its Righteousness (6:33)

VI. The Relationships of Kingdom Citizens
Matthew 7:1-12

A. Relationships to One Another (7:1-6)
   1. Judging (7:1-2)
   2. Hypocrisy (7:3-5)
   3. Discretion (7:6)
B. Relationship to God (7:7-11)
   1. Persistence in Prayer (7:7-8)
   2. Confidence in Prayer (7:9-11)
C. The Golden Rule: Ideal Reciprocal Relationships (7:12)

VII. The Commitment of Kingdom Citizens
Matthew 7:13-27

A. The Narrow and Wide Gates (7:13-14)
   1. The Choice
   2. The Outcome

B. A Tree and Its Fruit (7:15-23)
   1. False Prophets
   2. The Judgment
C. The Wise and Foolish Builders (7:24-27)

VIII. Conclusion: Jesus' Words for Today
Matthew 7:28-29
A. Who Is This Teacher?
B. The Teacher in Matthew's Gospel
   1. A Worker of Miracles
   2. Son of Man
   3. Son of David
   4. Son of God
   5. Christ
   6. Lord
C. The Significance of Jesus' Teaching for Today

Notes

Chapter 1: What Is the Sermon on the Mount?

1. Joseph Klausner, *Jesus of Nazareth: His Life, Times and Teaching* (New York: Macmillan, 1929), 392-93.

Chapter 2: The Character and Influence of Kingdom Citizens

1. G.H.R. Horsley, *New Documents Illustrating Early Christianity, 1979* (North Ryde: Macquarrie University, 1986), 4:170.

2. Frederick Dale Bruner, *The Christbook: A Historical/Theological Commentary: Matthew 1-12* (Waco, Tex.: Word, 1987), 137.

3. T.W. Manson, *The Sayings of Jesus* (London: SCM, 1949), 151.

4. Will Campbell, "On Silencing Our Finest," *Christianity and Crisis 45* (Sept. 26, 1985), 340.

Chapter 3: The Righteousness of Kingdom Citizens

1. Ap. Gell. x. 23.

2. Babylonian Talmud Ta'anit 24a.

3. de Cult Fem ii. 2.

4. One thing that prevented divorce was the sum settled on before the marriage, which was to be paid to the wife if she were divorced. It was not a large sum and would hardly provide a lifetime income. It usually would tide a wife over for only a year or so.

5. Mishnah Gittin 9:3.

6. Mishnah Baba Quamma 9:6.

7. Simon of Cyrene was "compelled" by the Roman soldiers to carry Jesus' crossbar (Matt. 27:32).

8. Manson, *The Sayings of Jesus, 160.*

9. Solomon Zeitlin, *The Jewish Sources of the Sermon on the Mount* (New York: Ktav, 1969), xxv.

10. A.M. Hunter, *A Pattern for Life: An Exposition of the Sermon on the Mount* (Philadelphia: The Westminster Press, 1965), 62.

11. Paul Hinnebusch, *St. Matthew's Earthquake: Judgment and Discipleship in the Gospel of Matthew* (Ann Arbor, Mich.: Servant Books, 1980), 45.

Chapter 4: The Genuineness of Kingdom Citizens

1. A.B. Bruce, *Commentary on the Synoptic Gospels* in the *Expositor's Greek Testament*, ed. W. R. Nicoll (London: Hodder, 1897), 176.

2. Edward Schweizer, *The Good News According to Matthew*, trans. D. E. Green (Atlanta: John Knox, 1975), 144.

3. Robert Gundry makes the entertaining suggestion that it may mean to slip in the gift unobtrusively with the right hand alone rather than to use both hands in a manner designed to catch the attention of others. See R. H. Gundry, *Matthew* (Grand Rapids: Eerdmans, 1982), 102.

4. John R.W. Stott, *Christian Counter-Culture: The Message of the Sermon on the Mount* (Downers Grove, Ill.: InterVarsity, 1978), 132.

5. See G. Delling, "Battarizo *Battalogeo,*" in *Theological Dictionary of the New Testament*, ed. by G. Kittel, trans. by G. Bromiley, 10 vols. (Grand Rapids, Mich.: Eerdmans, 1964), 1:597.

6. See Krister Stendahl, "Matthew," in *Peake's Commentary on the Bible*, ed. M. Black and H.H. Rowley (New York: Nelson, 1962), 778-79.

7. John Calvin observed a parallel with the Ten Commandments: first, outlining our duty to God and second, our con-

cern for others. Also see Robert H. Mounce, *Matthew* (San Francisco: Harper & Row, 1985), 53; and F.W. Beare, *The Gospel According to Matthew* (San Francisco: Harper and Row 1981), 175.

8. F.F. Bruce, *Matthew* (London: Scripture Union, 1970), 21.

9. Manson, *Sayings of Jesus*, 169.

10. See W. Foerster, "Epiousios," in *Theological Dictionary of the New Testament*, ed. by G. Kittel, trans. by G. Bromiley, 10 vols. (Grand Rapids, Mich.: Eerdmans, 1964), 2:599-600.

11. Gundry, *Matthew*, 111.

Chapter 5: The Security of Kingdom Citizens

1. D. Martin Lloyd-Jones, *Studies in the Sermon on the Mount* (Grand Rapids, Mich.: Eerdmans, 1960), 142-43.

2. Frank Stagg, *Studies in Luke's Gospel* (Nashville: Convention Press, 1967), 91.

Chapter 6: The Relationships of Kingdom Citizens

1. D.A. Carson, "Matthew," in *The Expositor's Bible Commentary*, ed. F. E. Gaebelein (Grand Rapids, Mich.: Zondervan, 1984), 8:183.

2. Stott, *Christian Counter-Culture*, 177.

3. David Wenham, *The Parables of Jesus* (Downers Grove, Ill.: InterVarsity, 1989), 174-75.

4. F.F. Bruce, *The Hard Sayings of Jesus* (Downers Grove, Ill.: InterVarsity, 1983), 87.

5. Stott, *Christian Counter-Culture*, 184.

6. Stanley D. Toussaint, *Behold the King: A Study of Matthew* (Portland: Multnomah, 1980), 114-15.

7. William Barclay, *The Gospel of Matthew* (Philadelphia: Westminster, 1963), 1:276-77.

8. Myron S. Augsburger, *Matthew* (Waco, Tex.: Word, 1982), 99.

9. It is very surprising, however, that many early Christians referred to a negative form of the rule. The Western text

of Acts 15:29 has the negative form, as do the *Didache* (1–2) Theophilus, Irenaeus, and Tertullian.

10. R.T. France, *Matthew,* TNTC (Grand Rapids, Mich.: Eerdmans, 1985), 145-46.

Chapter 7: Commitment of Kingdom Citizens

1. Mounce, *Matthew,* 64.

2. Cited by Mounce, ibid.

3. Richard B. Gardner, *Matthew,* BCBC (Scottdale, Penn.: Herald, 1991), 136.

4. Stott, *Christian Counter-Culture, 196.*

5. A.T. Robertson, "Matthew," *Word Pictures in the New Testament* (Nashville: Broadman, 1930), 1:62. He notes that wolves are far more dangerous than the dogs and pigs (7:6).

6. Ibid.

7. Robert A. Guelich, *The Sermon on the Mount: A Foundation for Understanding* (Waco,Tex.: Word, 1982), 410-11.

8. The imagery of the storms reflects the climatic conditions in Palestine. The country is dry most of the year, but following the autumn rains, sudden torrents may rush down dry ravines and carry away anything in their path. See Mounce, *Matthew,* 66-67.

9. John Calvin, *Commentary on a Harmony of the Evangelists, Matthew, Mark and Luke,* 1558; trans. A.W. Morrison, eds. T.F. and D.W. Torrance (Grand Rapids, Mich.: Eerdmans, 1972), 242.

Chapter 8: Jesus' Words for Today

1. R.T. France, *Matthew: Evangelist and Teacher* (Grand Rapids, Mich.: Zondervan, 1989), 306.

2. For powerful applications of Jesus' words for today, see C.L. Blomberg, *Matthew,* NAC (Nashville: Broadman, 1992), 94-133.

Selected Bibliography

Albright, W. F. and C. S. Mann. *Matthew.* Garden City, N.Y.: Doubleday, 1971.

Augsburger, Myron S. *Matthew.* Waco, Tex.: Word, 1982.

Barbieri, Louis A. "Matthew." *The Bible Knowledge Commentary,* New Testament Edition. Edited by John F. Walvoord and Roy B. Zuck. Wheaton, Ill.: Victor, 1983.

Barclay, William. *The Gospel of Matthew.* 2 vols. Philadelphia: Westminster, 1975.

Blomberg, Craig L. *Interpreting the Parables.* Downers Grove, Ill.: IVP, 1990.

————. *Matthew.* NAC. Nashville: Broadman, 1992.

Boice, James. *The Sermon on the Mount.* Grand Rapids, Mich.: Zondervan, 1972.

Broadus, John. *Commentary on the Gospel of Matthew.* Valley Forge, Penn.: American Baptist Publication Society, 1886.

Bruce, A. B. "The Gospel According to Matthew." *The Expositor's Greek Testament.* London: Hodder, 1897.

Bruce, F. F. *Matthew.* London: Scripture Union, 1970.

————. *The Hard Sayings of Jesus.* Downers Grove, Ill.: IVP, 1983.

Bruner, Frederick Dale. *The Christbook: Matthew 1–12.* Waco, Tex.: Word, 1987.

Calvin, John. *Matthew, Mark, and Luke.* Edited by T. F. Torrance and D. W. Torrance. Grand Rapids, Mich.: Eerdmans, 1972.

Carson, D. A. "Matthew." *The Expositor's Bible Commentary.* Vol. 8. Edited by F. E. Gaebelein. Grand Rapids, Mich.: Zondervan, 1984.

———. *The Sermon on the Mount.* Grand Rapids, Mich.: Baker, 1978.

Davies, W. D. *The Setting of the Sermon on the Mount.* Cambridge: University Press, 1963.

——— and Dale Allison. *Matthew.* Vol. 1. ICC. Edinburg: T & T Clark, 1988.

Fenton, J. C. *The Gospel of St. Matthew.* PNTC. New York: Penguin, 1963.

Filson, Floyd V. *A Commentary on the Gospel According to St. Matthew.* HNTC. New York: Harper, 1960.

France, R. T. *Matthew.* TNTC. Grand Rapids, Mich.: Eerdmans, 1985.

Gardner, Richard B. *Matthew.* BCBC. Scottdale, Penn.: Herald, 1991.

Guelich, Robert A. *The Sermon on the Mount.* Waco, Tex.: Word, 1982.

Gundry, Robert H. *Matthew: A Commentary on His Literary and Theological Art.* Grand Rapids, Mich.: Eerdmans, 1981.

Hendriksen, William. *The Gospel of Matthew.* Grand Rapids, Mich.: Baker, 1973.

Hill, David. *The Gospel of Matthew.* NCB. Grand Rapids, Mich.: Eerdmans, 1972.

Hinnebusch, Paul. *St. Matthew's Earthquake: Judgment and Discipleship in the Gospel of Matthew.* Ann Arbor, Mich.: Servant, 1980.

Hobbs, Herschel H. *An Exposition of the Gospel of Matthew.* Grand Rapids, Mich.: Baker, 1965.

Hunter, A. M. *A Pattern for Life: An Exposition of the Sermon on the Mount.* Philadelphia: Westminster, 1965.

Jeremias, Joachim. *The Prayers of Jesus.* Translated by J. Bowden and C. Burchard. London: SCM, 1967.

Kingsbury, Jack Dean. *Matthew.* Philadelphia: Fortress, 1977.

Klausner, Joseph. *Jesus of Nazareth: His Life Times, and Teaching.* New York: Macmillan, 1929.

Kraybill, Donald B. *The Upside-Down Kingdom.* Scottdale, Penn.: Herald, 1978.

Ladd, George E. *The Presence of the Future.* Grand Rapids, Mich.: Eerdmans, 1974.

Lenski, R. C. H. *Interpretation of St. Matthew's Gospel.* Columbus, Ohio: Lutheran Book Concern, 1932.

Lewis, C. S. *God in the Dock.* Grand Rapids, Mich.: Eerdmans, 1970.

Lloyd-Jones, D. M. *Studies in the Sermon on the Mount.* 2 vols. Grand Rapids, Mich.: Eerdmans, 1959-60.

Maclaren, Alexander. *Expositions of Holy Scripture.* Vol. 6. Grand Rapids, Mich.: Baker, reprint, 1974.

Manson, T. W. *The Sayings of Jesus.* London: SCM, 1957.

Morgan, G. Campbell. *The Gospel According to Matthew.* Old Tappan, N.J.: Revell, 1929.

Mounce, Robert H. *Matthew.* GNC. San Francisco: Harper and Row, 1985.

Plummer, Alfred. *An Exegetical Commentary on the Gospel According to St. Matthew.* London: Scott, 1915.

Robertson, A. T. "Matthew and Mark." *Word Pictures in the New Testament*. Vol. 1, Nashville: Broadman, 1930.

Schweizer, Eduard. *The Good News According to Matthew*. Atlanta: John Knox, 1975.

Smith, Robert H. *Matthew*. ACNT. Minneapolis, Minn.: Augsburg, 1989.

Spurgeon, C. H. *The Gospel of the Kingdom: A Popular Exposition of Matthew*. London: Passmore and Alabaster, 1893.

Stagg, Frank. *Studies in Luke's Gospel*. Nashville: Convention, 1967.

Stendahl, Krister. "Matthew." *Peake's Commentary on the Bible*. Edited by M. Black and H. H. Rowley. New York: Nelson, 1962.

Stott, John R. W. *Christian Counter-Culture: The Message of the Sermon on the Mount*. TBST. Downers Grove, Ill.: IVP, 1978.

Tasker, R. V. G. *The Gospel According to St. Matthew*. TNTC. Grand Rapids, Mich.: Eerdmans, 1961.

Toussant, Stanley D. *Behold the King: A Study of Matthew*. Portland, Oreg.: Multnomah, 1980.

Vos, Howard F. *Matthew*. Grand Rapids, Mich.: Zondervan, 1982.

Walvoord, John F. *Matthew: Thy Kingdom Come*. Chicago: Moody, 1974.

Wenham, David. *The Parables of Jesus*. Downers Grove, Ill.: IVP, 1989.